Save Your Kids...Now!

The Revolutionary Guide to Helping Youth Conquer Today's Challenges

Save Your Kids...Now!

The Revolutionary Guide to Helping
Youth Conquer Today's Challenges

Douglas Haddad, Ph.D.

iUniverse, Inc.
New York   Bloomington

SAVE YOUR KIDS...NOW!: The Revolutionary Guide To Helping Youth Conquer Today's Challenges is intended to provide helpful and informative material for adults to understand health and lifestyle challenges that school-aged children may encounter and provide solutions for helping them overcome any lifestyle challenge in order to achieve mind, body, and spirit wellness. This book does not provide medical advice. One must consult a medical or health professional before engaging in any new exercise, nutrition, supplementation, or wellness program.

The author specifically disclaims all responsibility for any liability or losses, personal or otherwise, that is included as a consequence, directly or indirectly, of the use and application of any of the information that is provided in this book.

iUniverse books may be ordered through booksellers or by contacting:

iUniverse
1663 Liberty Drive
Bloomington, IN 47403
www.iuniverse.com
1-800-Authors (1-800-288-4677)

Because of the dynamic nature of the Internet, any Web addresses or links contained in this book may have changed since publication and may no longer be valid. The views expressed in this work are solely those of the author and do not necessarily reflect the views of the publisher, and the publisher hereby disclaims any responsibility for them.

ISBN: 978-1-4401-5303-7 (sc)
ISBN: 978-1-4401-5305-1 (dj)
ISBN: 978-1-4401-5304-4 (ebook)
Printed in the United States of America

iUniverse rev. date: 07/21/2009

Contents

ACKNOWLEDGMENTS

First and foremost, I would like to take this opportunity to thank my wife Laura Haddad for inspiring me to utilize different perspectives throughout this book along with her contributions as an editor. I would like to thank my parents, Michael and Donna Haddad, grandparents, Joseph and Clare Petrucelli, and my uncle, Joseph J. Petrucelli, for their endless support in all of my endeavors. My family is my greatest inspiration and all that I hope to achieve will be evidenced through their dedication in my life. I wish to bring light to people's lives including my family, friends, students I teach, readers of my books, listeners who tune in to my radio show, audiences who watch my acting, piano, and singing performances, and new encounters that I make throughout my life. I wish all who read this book to be fueled with the knowledge and confidence necessary to help young people achieve great mind, body, and spirit heights.

Introduction
SAVE YOUR KIDS... NOW!

"It is no sin to attempt and fail. The only sin is not to make the attempt."

-SUELLEN FRIED
(author, speaker)

Social scientists have proposed a number of theories explaining the development of the individual. Recently there has been a rapid growth of interest in the study of childhood, the developmental time period in humans between infancy and adulthood, and its significance in adult development. Sociologist, psychologist, and philosopher George Herbert Mead understood the "self" as the basis of humanity that develops through social experience. He says that humans begin the understanding of their world through play. The child takes on different roles that she/he observes in the "adult society" and gains an understanding of general, acceptable norms within that group or setting (Benokraitis, 2008). Later on in life, through maturation, an individual can take on that role — whether it is a teacher, doctor, police officer, or criminal.

Socialization is defined as "the process of acquiring the language, accumulated knowledge, attitudes, beliefs, and values of one's society and culture and learning the social and interpersonal skills needed to function effectively in society" (Benokraitis, 2008). Childhood experiences play a large role in the socialization and development of an individual. Understanding this critical phase of life will help us best understand our lives and the problems that persist in society. I have decided to focus on the root of challenges existing in society and on obtaining and providing viable solutions to help youth. Children should have the best opportunity for success early on and face the music in life with a "whole strength" that is their own so they can grow with the prospect of becoming self-actualized adults.

Today's cohort of children has been proclaimed as the generation without restraint. They have been coined "over the top" in just about all meanings of the phrase. This group of children is said to take it to the extremes in terms of fashion, music, video games, cell phones, computers, junk food consumption, and overall risky behavior. We often hear the all too familiar narrative that "kids today aren't what they used to be." So, how in fact were the kids just before the turn of the century?

According to many elite journalists at the time, the kids of the 1990s were the "worst generation" appearing apathetic, asocial, and coldly murderous. At the time, Governor Gray Davis in California proposed a mandatory community service for college students, so they could regain their sense of the future and get back to the ethics earlier in the century (Males, 1999).

Examining the press reports in the 1930s indicates an ironic interpretation of "The Greatest Generation," the nickname given to the children of that era (Males, 1999):

- "This is a generation, numbering in the millions, that has gone so far in decay that it acts without thought of social responsibility."
- "They are youth gone loco: Villain is marijuana."
- "Drug-crazed teens have murdered entire families!"
- "High-school kids are armed and dangerous. Watch out for what they can get."
- "This generation of kids is rotting before our eyes."

Would it be foolhardy to state that today's youth is "Generation Z?" I would coin them the "Zoomers Generation." Taking the time and witness how these children interact on a personal and "cyberworldistic" level, you will see that what they desire is, often times, a click away. Communicating through a text message, watching video after video at one's computer, shopping for clothes online, downloading music and games, and "talking with and meeting friends" on the latest social networking websites are common to this generation of young people.

Although these children have virtually everything available at their fingertips, they still have the same needs as past generations of children where their expression of musical taste, clothing, games, and friends is really a call for love and acceptance. Sadly enough, much of their behaviors are expressed through fear and escape into the cyberworld. They lose opportunities to develop resiliency skills in learning how to handle adversity face-to-face. Has technology come so far to significantly decrease one's social skills, attention span, and overall wellness? Are children nowadays more illiterate than e-literate?

Blaming a whole generation of children and pointing fingers at bad behaviors when circumstances start to spiral out of control in our own society can be the worst thing that can be done. It is important to wake up and take notice of ourselves and recover some very vital functions that are being stripped from us. The search for solutions to worldly challenges starts from looking outside at the world around us. Just possibly, the "better behavior" represented by fairness, kindness, peace, love, cooperation, patience, respect, and trustworthiness that is desired is often lacking from our television programming, in video games, on the radio, in political arenas, in sporting events, and in other media outlets.

It is important to realize that parents, family members, teachers, administrators, counselors, social workers, psychologists, coaches, law enforcement, and mass media are at the forefront for impacting a child. All adults should look within themselves in regards to problems displayed by "a child." The "whole child" involves the social, physical, mental, and academic wellness of that child. Time and energy are required to help children progress through their life stages. Moreover, maintaining one's own well-being is necessary to help successfully guide a child.

It is important to challenge a young, vibrant individual to become an extraordinary person with unlimited potential to make a positive impact to change the world. Adults must do what is right regardless of time and money constraints because messages are constantly bombarding those watching and listening. In order for this revolution to take place, children must be encouraged, supported, listened to, played with, and educated by parents, teachers, and other adult figures.

For my entire life, I have been closely associated with children in some capacity as a classmate, friend, mentor, educator, coach, performance enhancement specialist, and inspirational speaker. I grew up and also worked with children from a wide variety of socioeconomic and ethnic backgrounds coming from a vast array of family dynamics. From early on in life I have encountered challenges that, at the time of occurrence, seemed insurmountable and never-ending. I couldn't understand why many of my peers would attempt to bring me down and make me feel less valued. I used to ask myself, "What did I do to deserve this? How can I stop them from doing that to me?"

I like to use the analogy that life is like a video game. A young person can obtain "power points" at different stages that can be added to one's account to help throughout life's journey. Parents, close family members, teachers, and other special adults are responsible for providing these "power points." Those who care to understand the daily challenges a child goes through and provide a safe, encouraging environment greatly influence the overall support given to a child. These individuals have been an outstanding support for me throughout the tumultuous transition from boyhood to adulthood. They have provided the stability for me to shine in the face of darkness, to rise above all adversity over the years, have greatly shaped what I have become today, and are largely responsible for my success.

Over the years I have witnessed many young individuals fall short of their potential for success and turn to risky, harmful behaviors that have negatively altered the course of their life. I have seen its effect not only on them, but also on their families. I constantly questioned why some individuals would "follow the crowd" and why others would "be the authors of their own life story." I would wonder why certain kids would care more about academics, friends, others' feelings, be motivated about life, internalize morals and values, stand up for themselves, and/or have determination to succeed while others would not.

The basic premise of why I chose to write this book was to provide adults with an understanding of the root of challenges that plague society, how these are linked to childhood, and the power that adult figures have in their control to be the solution for helping today's youth. The information provided in this book is the result of qualitative research, a review of scientific research, and first-hand practical situations along with successful solutions implemented over the course of more than a decade interacting as an adult figure in children's lives.

In the first chapter, you will be asked to take a journey back to your school days and recall the day-to-day pressures experienced to better understand yourself and a child. Specific strategies are discussed for educating a child on the basics of life including setting up a solid foundation and providing expectations for proper behavior, helping a child gain self-confidence, emphasizing the value of self-discipline for life success, creating good life habits, and getting a child physically active. There are strategies provided on how to communicate positive messages when the situation may or may not be so positive and how to get a child motivated and always striving to do her/his best. In addition, the power of family and how it greatly affects the socialization of a child are discussed. The chapter concludes with strategies presented for adults to best understand and handle situations of crisis with children.

In chapter two, a super health program is designed for adults to help guide a child on the road to success. Healthy foods to eat and unhealthy foods to avoid are highlighted. Customized strength training programs and fun, heart-pumping activities are provided. Recreation advocates have addressed a concern for the lack of formal physical education in schools, poor facilities, and limited opportunities for children to engage in organized sports after school.

Chapter three addresses topics that many young people get mixed up with that can render serious consequences. Social workers have made reference to a higher prevalence of depression, violent behaviors, eating disorders, destructive self-inflicting behaviors, thoughts of suicide, and drug and alcohol abuse. Provided are specific prevention and intervention strategies for adults to utilize with children before situations turn serious and also if they have already become severe. Real-life case studies are presented along with effective solutions addressing these topics. The root causes of these problems and plans to best solve the main ones of concern for you are discussed. This chapter also focuses on the risk factors, causes, effective reduction, and best prevention of widespread violence in our communities.

Various media outlets display themes of violence and attempt to specifically target children. Bullying is a key factor in many kids dropping out of school, resorting to violence in the schools, at home, and in the communities, and/or committing suicide. Moreover, the choices expressed by children on what to wear, what music to listen to, what movies to watch, choice of friends, what interests to have, and activities to enjoy are communication lines attempting to find a place to fit in within our world.

Young people are vulnerable to exhibited mass media ideal body images. Drastic measures can be taken by youth in order to achieve what is valued and propagated by society. The serious nature of eating disorders and the use of anabolic steroids are underscored along with specific strategies to help encourage healthy eating and exercise habits and an overall healthy lifestyle. When we flip through magazines, catalogs, look at billboards, and watch television, we see that the message given in society is spoken loud and clear. "Sex sells!" These images that girls must be thin, and boys must be muscular, are portrayed in the media on a continuous basis and are unrealistic and unhealthy.

I conclude the chapter on the health and lifestyle challenges targeting today's society with a focus on one of the major challenges globally affecting today's youth and adults: the obesity pandemic. The potential long term physical, social, and emotional outcomes and early intervention strategies to help prevent life long obesity are revealed.

In chapter four, a big picture is portrayed for how a child's lasting behaviors are greatly affected by adults' daily actions. There are specific ways provided in which all adults can demonstrate and reinforce positive messages for children.

The final chapter of the book is addressed to the beloved child within all of us. To find that child is to find the beauty in life. It is important to realize that we are given the power of decision to create a world that we choose. It is important to understand that the world we live in is merely a reflection of ourselves. Desiring change for something better in this world begins from within. Focusing on helping a child will help change the world significantly and nurture woman/mankind indefinitely.

The title of this book *Save Your Kids...Now!* states that there is no time to waste when helping a child. It is the duty of all adults to step forward and help the younger generation overcome health and lifestyle obstacles involving widespread violence, increased rate of suicides, a global obesity epidemic, body image issues, and addictive behaviors including gambling, sex, alcohol, smoking, prescription drugs, substance abuse, etc.

Depicting a clear perspective of our society and how we are impacted is a major goal that I intend to achieve by the conclusion of this book. How we perceive and address these pressing concerns will determine the future of our global society. Knowing what we have within our power to understand ourselves and how to use that for the future are ultimate keys for a better world. Let us now take a journey into society and find the answers to help youth overcome challenges along their unique paths of life.

"You can make the picture bright or dark.
The point is that YOU CAN!
THERE ARE NO MORE EXCUSES...
SAVE YOUR KIDS...NOW!"

"There are only two ways to live life. One is as though nothing is a miracle. The other is as though everything is a miracle."

-ALBERT EINSTEIN
(physicist)

Chapter I
TOOLS FOR UNDERSTANDING TODAY'S CHALLENGES

"Some people regard discipline as a chore. For me, it is a kind of order that sets me free to fly."

-JULIE ANDREWS
(award-winning actress, singer, author)

The assumption that life has its fair share of ups and downs would be reasonable. Wouldn't you think? Presuming that children will find their way throughout life and make it through unscathed is highly dependent upon many factors. One fact that is for certain is that children will experience. What they will experience varies from person-to-person and situation-to-situation.

Caring adults help foster a child's emotions and encourage communication and self-expression. They help a child create healthy lifestyle habits that become internalized to her/his identity. Parents and educators are prominent figures responsible for a child's protection, security, care, and feelings. It is throughout childhood and adolescence that children may need extra help to cope with a crisis.

The following tools in this chapter are vital to the understanding of various crises that children experience throughout their growth and development. With this understanding and knowledge, problems can be prevented from occurring, trouble can be spotted before it becomes a problem, and strategies can be utilized to help work through a problem if it takes place.

1.   REMEMBERING WHAT IT WAS LIKE TO BE THEIR AGE

The question "How was school today?" may very well be the most frequently asked and least answered question by parents and children, respectively. As children get older, the description of their day becomes less and less detailed. What parents are really asking, especially as they get older, is not how school was, but rather "How is your life going?" Often times, the response shrinks down to "Fine," which really means what?

Since adults went to school when they were kids, one would assume that they would best understand what a child is feeling in school. However, I have seen many parents out of touch with their children and removed from their educational experiences. They focus heavily on grades and less on day-to-day pressures that have such a powerful influence on a child's overall well-being.

There are thousands of questions that could be asked about your days at school. Asking the question "How was your day today?" seems to be an apparently complex question to answer. The importance of listening to children to best understand them starts with understanding your days spent as a student and recalling more than just selective, dreamy memories, but also the day-to-day pressures that affected your perceptions on life and how that impacted you positively or negatively.

> ➤ Are these memories fond or would you like to forget about the past?

> ➤ What moments of inspiration did you have that sparked a change in the course of your life?

> ➤ Do you wish that you had done something different in various situations with friends, bullies, or sports teammates?

> ➤ How would you have changed events?

What emotions are rekindled?

Was school boring for you growing up?

Did you look forward to going to school each morning?

How did you feel when the bus arrived to pick you up each day?

How did you feel riding the bus in the morning? in the afternoon?

How did you feel at the bus waiting area near home? at the school?

Do you remember walking into class and seeing your worst enemy staring at you?

Do you remember the difference a teacher you liked or hated had on you?

Do you remember a teacher that you liked a lot and how she/he made you feel?

Did you look forward to going to gym class? math class? science class? art class? history class? etc.?

How did it feel to sit in those hard seats all day?

Did you look forward to eating lunch with your peers?

How did you feel when you had to change your clothes in front of others at gym class?

Were you afraid of being picked last for games?

Did you ever write notes to friends in school? To whom? In what class did you write them?

How did you feel when you had to show your parents your report card?

Were you proud of your efforts?

Did you wish that your parents would understand you better growing up?

Did you feel loved and cared for by others?

Why did you choose the friends that you had growing up?

Was there someone who you were afraid to face in school and tried to avoid?

Did you worry about dressing to impress others?

How did you feel right before going to sports practice after school?

How did you feel when you were being laughed at or made fun of by a select person or group of people?

Were you nervous walking in the halls from class to class?

Did your parents care about how your days were at school? How did it make you feel?

Did you feel embarrassed to be around your parents when you were with your friends?

As a public school teacher, I deal with children who come from different backgrounds having their own unique, personal needs. I attempt to relate to children by conjuring up my past and putting myself back in school experiencing how I felt. I am fortunate to say that my recollections of growing up are quite clear and I recall the smells and textures of the classrooms, locker rooms, restrooms, library, and gym and remember my inner feelings, fears, joys, and dreams as if it were yesterday that I was a student at school.

Hearing from parents over the years that their children enjoyed my class and that I was their favorite teacher meant a great deal, not to me personally satisfying my ego, but rather knowing that students experienced a safe, pleasant feeling in my classroom throughout the school year. Most importantly, this signifies the importance of never forgetting what it was like to be their age and utilizing that knowledge to help children in the best possible manner.

Being able to relate to, understand, and make a difference in someone's life require an individual or group who can closely relate to a child's experience. True self-worth and understanding of one self is developed over a lifetime of experiences. As children grow, they experience various highs and lows and are looking to parents, teachers, counselors, coaches, mass media figures, etc. who can best understand and identify with them in helping to guide them through these ever-changing times, even if they do not verbally express for help. Youth can be best serviced by remembering what it was like to be in their shoes.

2 FAMILY'S ROLE FOR THE SOCIALIZATION OF AN INDIVIDUAL

In the process of socializing a child, adults can implicitly or explicitly pass on their own values, attitudes, and prejudices. Parents of any color should not offend any particular race and display hatred due to past history or dealings with specific groups of people. For example, parents should feel a responsibility to educate their child on the history of their culture and discuss contemporary issues about what it means to be that particular ethnic background in today's society. Early in a child's life, it is important not to fall into the vicious circle trap where one feels that a group of people should be owed something from another group. All ethnic groups are important and unique, yet we are all biologically created from the same chemical substances, and deserve equal respect and equal opportunity.

It is important for us to facilitate a child to communicate her/his feelings openly and honestly. We should never say to a child, "boys don't cry" and prevent these emotions from being manifested. The lexicon of messages that we send to children forthrightly, subtly, and through interactions with family members, friends, and strangers has a direct impact on them. Being interested in a child, answering the questions, explaining life's phenomena, and paying attention to what is going on each day speaks volumes that "YOU CARE!"

The art of parenting

Parenting style has been found to predict child well-being in the domains of social competence, academic performance, psychosocial development, and problematic behavior. Two important elements on parenting include parental responsiveness, which involves providing love, warmth, support, and fostering a sense of individuality in the child and parental demandingness, which involves the type of discipline used and demands/expectations for responsible behavior. Parenting styles such as being indulgent, authoritative, authoritarian, and uninvolved greatly affect long-term child behavior (Weiss and Schwarz, 1996).

Research based on parent interviews, child reports, and parent observations consistently indicates the benefits of authoritative parenting where there is an equal level of responsiveness and demandingness. Authoritative parenting predicts good psychosocial outcomes and less problematic behaviors for adolescents in all ethnic groups studied (African-, Asian-, European-, and Hispanic-Americans), but it is associated with academic performance only among European Americans and, to a lesser extent, Hispanic Americans. Researchers have argued that observed ethnic differences in the association of parenting style with child outcomes may be due to differences in social context, parenting practices, or the cultural meaning of specific dimensions of parenting style (Weiss and Schwarz, 1996).

Raising a child takes a great amount of time, effort, and patience in teaching them how to become responsible citizens, to have self-control, to live up to societal and cultural expectations, and to exhibit the proper values in life. Conversations centered on educational issues are very important for the future success of a child. Parents who provide children with emotional support and encourage them to value education have higher achieving kids at school (Darling and Steinberg, 1993).

Parent-child interactions, in regards to homework, stem from parents' cultural knowledge about school. Moreover, family socialization practices differ around the world. Chinese families use personal storytelling as a medium of socialization (Miller et al., 1997). This culture is deeply rooted in the Confucian tradition, which places an emphasis on proper moral and social standards (Chao, 1994). They see shame as a virtue and place a high order on strict discipline from an early age and fulfilling social obligations. American families see story telling as more entertaining and lesson learning (Miller et al., 1997).

There are two major groups that have been characterized as integral to a child's socialization. The primary group, typified by close, long-lasting, loving, and nurturing relationships, is necessary in order for young individuals to be happy, healthy, and to feel secure. Family and close friends comprise this group, which functions as the strongest working units in a child's life. The secondary group is characterized by impersonal and short-term relationships in which people work together on common tasks or activities. These are individuals that also affect the socialization of a child. Members of this group have less, if any, emotional ties to the individual including mass media outlets, classmates (except for close friends), most teachers, professors, and other people who will inevitably come and go in a child's life. This group will usually listen politely to conversation, but will not have a vested interest in the "whole child" — will not care to hear all of the details of a youth's life, and will not be available for that person in the case of an emergency (Benokraitis, 2008).

A major goal of most children in school is to "be accepted and fit in." The important goal of a parent is to guide a child down the path of least destruction and greatest fulfillment without her/him getting hurt socially, emotionally, and/or physically. Parents have a unique task — to help guide children in a positive direction without directing their every move. It is important for a child to gain a sense of independence and responsibility taking ownership of her/his actions and seeing the benefits and consequences for such doings.

Here is a sample discussion that parents can use, in part or in whole, to communicate with their children addressing the pressures to be "cool at school":

"You will see and experience yourself and your friends changing throughout your school career. Some of your classmates may choose to experiment with drugs, alcohol, and smoking thinking that these are the cool things to do. Your "friends" may try to persuade you into doing these things together. These people are not your true friends and are not looking out for your best interest. You may think it to be difficult to say the word "NO" with the fear of rejection or embarrassment and how you might look in the eyes of everyone. They may try to hurt your feelings making you feel bad or uncool for not doing what THEY want you to do and keep asking you to do what THEY want until you break down and fall to their pressure. It is important to understand that they are only hurting themselves the more they "try to hurt you." It may not seem like it at first, but this is all short-lived and becomes old quick. No matter what these people say to you, these behaviors will catch up later on in their own lives. They just don't see it yet, unfortunately. Once you stand up for yourself and hold your ground, you will suddenly gain a strength from within that will carry with you the rest of your life. It may feel strange at first to stand up to these people, but other people will see this. Maybe not right away, but definitely over time you will gain respect from your peers and your inner strength will shine through. It may be hard to believe that one day, you will actually be as old as your parents! You may think that's not for a long, long time anyway. It's true, yet it happens quicker than one can imagine. How many of my childhood friends do I keep in contact with now? For

that matter, conduct an interview with many adults and find out how many regularly communicate with their elementary, middle, or high school friends. I bet that very few adults are still in contact with many of their old friends from school. Think about what it means for you. Do not pay attention to what ANY ONE of your classmates thinks of you. YOU make the healthy choices in your own life to keep building a strong future so YOU can do and be anything that YOU want to be and not live someone else's life! It is your mind, your body, and YOU are in control of doing what is right and thinking your way to success!"

It is important to realize that it is not just the words spoken, but also the behaviors of parents that are the examples in which children regularly follow. The socialization of a child takes place through contributions of both primary and secondary groups. In some cultures, individuals marry quite early in their teen years and are considered adults while in Western countries, many people remain dependent on their parents into and throughout their twenties. Families must engage a child at an early age in the socialization process and be aware of all of the factors that contribute to a child's understanding of her/his world in order to best help a child become a responsible, respected, and contributing member of society.

3. EDUCATING ONE ON THE BASICS

From an early age children should be educated on what is appropriate conduct for different circumstances. It is necessary to provide children with the expectations for proper behavior towards family members, strangers, teachers, and classmates.

How do you get a child to behave appropriately?

Reward a child for a good deed done well. Children tend to continue a behavior when they are rewarded. This is one of the most frequent forms of control. However, many parents are unaware of the consequences to different types of rewards. Material rewards such as money, candy, food, and toys can result in a child coming to expect a reward for every accomplishment and will not carry out the desired task without one. Social rewards such as verbal praise, play, or talk pose a problem in that a child may become more attached to the reward than to the behavior and as a result demand sociability in return for performance (Collins and Coltrane, 2000).

Although rewards work fine for B.F. Skinner's laboratory rats, they do not necessarily work for humans. Various studies suggest that children praised for doing well at something were less interested for pursuing it, or did less well at later tasks. Dr. Joan Grusec, a University of Toronto psychology professor, found that children who were frequently praised by their mothers for displays of generosity tended to be less generous on an everyday basis than other children (Kohn, 1999).

Rewards can come in a variety of positive reinforcements that do not have to be announced to a child.

What are some examples of rewards?

- Involvement in deciding on a special meal during the week.
- Earning "special points" towards a toy or game of some sort.
- Earning time to play a favorite game.
- A choice of a favorite book to read.
- A choice of a movie to watch.
- Involvement in choosing a fun activity to play as a family.

Eat dinner as a family and discuss the day's events. Research has shown that children who eat dinner each night with their parents have stronger ties to their family. Two critical goals for a child are the development to have self-initiative to complete schoolwork, homework, and at home chores in a timely, efficient manner each day without being told to do so repeatedly and the ability to make good decisions within a peer group (Farias, 2007).

If things do not appear to be working and a child is not complying with the rules and expectations that are set forth, then should punishment be used as a last resort? This is a delicate situation that is child-specific. Various factors to take into account that will help you make the best decision include:

- Parents' actions are a model for their child.
- The child's specific likes and dislikes.
- The child's unique personality.

Disciplining a child should be used as an opportunity for education by reinforcing what is expected. Physical punishment can send mixed signals to a child about what is appropriate, expected conduct. A child is not being taught a good behavior that is desired, but rather experiencing an unwanted behavior. This form of punishment (such as spankings) has been used to stop bad behavior. When used on multiple occasions, this can lead to child abuse — which can aggravate and precipitate other unwanted and aggressive behaviors.

Providing poor examples for youth will affect them adversely. Rather than looking for a temporary solution for any such problems, it is important to demonstrate patience, understanding, fairness, and consistency in handling situations.

- Choose a designated area of the house that is safe, yet free of distraction for a timeout.
- Address the behavior as bad, not the child.
- Discuss what the child has done, what she/he should have done, and what she/he will do in the future.
- As opposed to taking away privileges from the child, refrain from granting special rewards that would have been given for doing the right thing.

- Pick your battles. One of the best ways to encourage good behavior is to hold your standards high and expect good behavior. Impart a policy that states the expectations to be followed clearly.
- Try active ignoring of a child's bad behavior (unless it poses a threat to either the child or someone else). This method of managing children is particularly effective in reducing the tantrums of toddlers and preschoolers. Admonishing or giving attention to a child while she/he is having an outburst may unintentionally reward that undesired behavior. Provide attention to a child only when she/he calms down. Be sure a child's bad behavior does not get her/him a material or social reward.

Effective discipline involves more than rewards and punishments. Children must internalize an understanding of right and wrong and be taught effective strategies to solve problems. They should feel valued and have a positive perception of others in society. These are just some of the many highly useful methods that parents and other adults can utilize in helping to educate and grow a child into becoming responsible, productive individuals.

4. GAINING SELF-CONFIDENCE AND LEADERSHIP

In the book, *Leading Minds: An Anatomy of Leadership*, Howard Gardner defines a leader as an individual (or, rarely, a set of individuals) who significantly affects the thoughts, feelings, and/or behaviors of a significant number of individuals (1995). Although some of today's leaders in society may not be seen in the most positive light, it is imperative for a child to witness the impact one can have as a good leader. For instance, it is unfortunate that the negative campaigning techniques used by politicians during election time are broadcast over the television and seen by millions of people as the way to win recognition. Dirty politics have long been the tactics used to gain popularity showcasing the opponent to be dishonest, corrupt, a criminal, and a cheat. This crude attack of the competition has demonstrated disrespect for many involved including the political competitor, her/his party, and supporters. Mostly, the offender is disrespecting herself/himself and her/his own family — at all costs.

In today's dynamic and largely unpredictable world, we rely on leadership at all levels to make decisions for our future as policymakers in our local communities and to make global decisions as it pertains to our involvement with other countries. For example, military leaders have organized groups of highly trained combatants to perform team-based leadership situations and make important decisions that they would carry out in wartime. These leaders have serious roles of establishing strategic plans of action and recreating battlefield scenarios. In this fast-paced setting, confident decision-making and leadership are a premium.

Individuals who understand how to relate to others through communicating and listening form positive relationships with others and are viewed as leaders. They refrain from attracting negative attention to themselves in various social encounters by interpreting social situations, learning how to make judgments, and taking into consideration the feelings of inadequacy and self-esteem of others. They view their own actions with how they will be perceived in comparison to their peers (Gardner, 1995).

It must not only be said, but also shown what it means to be self-confident on a regular basis. Determining one's life path is a challenging task at any stage of life, requiring an individual to make choices daily that will affect future choices to be made. During one's adolescent years, an individual has an added pressure to be accepted by peers — which largely influences one's self-esteem and self-image. Defining what "being popular" truly means rather than what is often portrayed through popular culture including television, music, fashion, advertising, hobbies, and sports is what is important for a child to learn before she/he decides to "follow a certain crowd" to be accepted/popular.

"Popular points" to emphasize with kids

- Believe in yourself and do what YOU KNOW is right no matter what others may think.
- Be proud of who you are and demonstrate confidence in making decisions.
- Be a courageous support and stand up for a friend in need.
- Be a team player who listens to others and demonstrates cooperation.
- Donate your time and/or money earned to a worthy cause.
- Be a camp counselor, mentor/tutor, and/or captain of a game/team at school.
- Listen to the teacher and do your homework. Knowledge is the key to a bright future.
- Offer to help around the house and at school.
- Ask for help when you need it.
- Get involved in an after school activity, club, and/or sports team to form new relationships.
- Make decisions with confidence and stick to them without any fear of rejection.

Strong-willed, confident people are important for the development and innovation of this world. There is a difference between being a team player who demonstrates cooperation with others' ideas and agreeing to do whatever someone else or a group wants to do — without taking one's own opinion into consideration. To be a leader requires that there are a group of followers. In regards to ethics and morals, a leader's actions can drastically affect others. As adults, we know that the different clicks in school fade away over time and that contact with former classmates becomes less and less prevalent as years progress.

It is important for children to realize that demonstrating respect for themselves and others will not be forgotten and will carry with them for a lifetime. Leading by example and being a good role model for youth are very important and should be underscored. Leaders are made, not born. It is the responsibility of primary caregivers to be effective leaders and to demonstrate for a child how to act appropriately towards others. This will offset any misinformation that is provided about values, roles, and family life in pop culture.

5. EMPHASIZING THE VALUE OF SELF-DISCIPLINE
FOR LIFE SUCCESS

Whether adults assume the role or not, they are fundamental guideposts that help pave the way for children to succeed in life.   Originating back around 500 B.C. in India, the art of Zen was one of the earliest documented strategic approaches for improving the quality of one's life through self-discipline, courage, and perseverance (What is Zen Buddhism, 2009). Today, society favors instant gratification over the long-term process for achieving a higher goal. Will power is a key ingredient that is necessary for attaining major success at almost any aspect of life — whether it be obtaining good grades, getting a fulfilling job, maintaining positive relationships with people, making a team, or being physically fit.

How can a child experience personal growth by becoming self-disciplined in a fast-paced, technologically booming society? There are many clubs and organizations that offer boys and girls the opportunity to laugh, play, develop their skills, express their feelings, and realize the value of their own worth.

Today, the Scout Movement is the largest voluntary youth organization with over 28 million boys and girls (Boy Scout Aims and Methods, 2006). Despite coming under some criticism for their strong adherence to traditional Christian morality, there is much we can learn from the principles imparted by this organization. The Boy Scouts of America promote universal goals that aim to help young people build their futures. All young individuals, regardless of race, religion, or sexual orientation, should be given equal opportunities for spiritual and character growth.

*AIMS OF SCOUTING

Character Development

> "This aim is to build self-reliance, self-discipline, self-confidence, and self-respect. The scout understands and improves oneself: his/her personal qualities, values, and outlook on life."

Citizenship Training

"This aim is to nurture respect of, participation in, and caring for community, nation, and world while fostering a commitment of service to others and an understanding of local, state, and national government. Citizenship refers to the scout's relationship to others — obligations to other people, to the society he/she lives in, and to the government of his/her society."

Personal Fitness

"This aim is to develop life-long physical, mental, emotional, and moral fitness. Fitness includes a healthy, strong body, a mind able to imagine and reason, and a spirit of courage, caring, and self-control."

*Source: www.boyscouttrail.com.

Here are some examples that adults can use as messages to help children become more self-disciplined:

- Use moderation as the key principle in eating junk food. Many children have control over their eating situations at school by choosing to bag it or buy it. For those children that receive free or reduced lunch, the good news is that the school lunch menus are offering more healthy choices. Children can be provided more nutritious choices that they agree to eat. Otherwise unknowingly and quite commonly, there may be daily trading of food at the lunch table and a child does not eat what is intended for her/him.

- Practice a daily routine of doing homework in the same place where parents are able to check completed homework. Children need this structure and routine in order to build a solid foundation for other aspects of their lives.

- Learn to say NO! Practice the refusal of temptations that can be harmful or hurtful. Peer pressures can seem like the worst thing in the world at the time, but with each "NO" expressed, a greater confidence is built that is seen by people. Taking the road less traveled will reward in a child's acquisition of inner strength and self-esteem.

• Avoid friendships that are one-sided in nature where the only thing that matters is NOT you. If a "friend" talks to you because she/he wants something from you all of the time, talks behind your back, and/or can not be trusted with a secret, then that person is not worthy of your friendship.

• Practice daily meditation. Sit still with eyes closed for 5 minutes and breathe with a relaxed in through the nose, out through the mouth action slowly. Focus on creating a vision for your dream to come true. See yourself as having complete control over your own life and achieving your goals. If negative thoughts appear, then release them kindly and smile. There are many benefits that are associated with this daily practice. To name a few of the many paybacks, one will experience an increase in self-confidence, feel more relaxed and less anxious, reduce overall stress, enhance the immune system, and help to better one's general health.

The root of most success or most evil early on in a child's life is their immediate caregivers. The messages implied directly and/or indirectly to children daily carry with them and become ingrained as part of a larger memory base to be applied in their own lives as they encounter situations. One of the greatest gifts that adults can provide children is the guidance towards their desires in life and teaching them that the results they produce in anything depend on their efforts and actions. To play an instrument well or become a better athlete, one has to form the correct practice habits and repeat them on a consistent basis to see results.

We must recognize that self-discipline is not something that one is born with, but is something learned over time. It takes consistent, proper practice of being aware of thoughts and behaviors and what actions are taken and if these actions lead to self-improvement and success. Children follow the advice and discipline demonstrated by adults in all situations and when the going gets tough, the disciplined individual perseveres and will not quit.

6. GETTING A CHILD PHYSICALLY ACTIVE

The National Association for Sport and Physical Education conducted a study that demonstrates a positive correlation between physically active children and academic performance. Reading and mathematics scores were matched with fitness scores of 353,000 fifth graders, 322,000 seventh graders, and 279,000 ninth graders (NASPE, 2002).

Key findings of the study include (NASPE, 2002):

- Higher achievement was associated with higher levels of fitness at each of the three grade levels measured.

- The relationship between academic achievement and fitness was greater in mathematics than in reading, particularly at higher fitness levels.

- Students who met minimum fitness levels in three or more physical fitness areas demonstrated the greatest gains in academic achievement at all three grade levels.

- Females demonstrated higher achievement than males, particularly at higher fitness levels.

Many young people today spend much of their time in front of a television or computer screen. One in four American children obtains an adequate amount of physical activity each day. The health benefits from exercise are extensive and include a reduction in stress, depression, anxiety, blood pressure, risk for adult-onset diseases, heart disease, body fat, the risk of obtaining cancer, bad cholesterol, a strengthening of the heart, lungs, and muscles throughout the body, increased flexibility, improved oxygen capacity, increased muscle endurance, enhanced mental acuity, an improved mood and sleep, etc (Fitness For Kids, 2007).

The American Academy of Orthopaedic Surgeons suggests exercise as a priority for all children and that childhood is a critical time for developing lifestyle habits that support bone growth (AAOS, 2003). Ninety percent of peak bone mass is acquired by age 18 in girls and age 20 in boys (Mann, 1999). A child's activity levels early on can greatly reduce her/his chances of developing osteoporosis when she/he gets older. Calcium-rich foods and weight-bearing exercises are highly recommended (Iannelli, 2007).

*Here are selected sources of calcium-rich foods recommended by the United States Department of Agriculture (USDA) for kids:

Food	Calcium (mg)	% DV *
Sardines, canned in oil, with bones, 3 oz.	324	32%
Cheddar cheese, 1 1/2 oz., shredded	306	31%
Milk, nonfat, 8 fl oz.	302	30%
Yogurt, plain, low fat, 8 oz.	300	30%
Milk, reduced fat (2% milk fat), no solids, 8 fl oz.	297	30%
Milk, whole (3.25% milk fat), 8 fl oz.	291	29%
Milk, buttermilk, 8 fl oz.	285	29%
Milk, lactose reduced, 8 fl oz. (content varies slightly according to fat content; average=300 mg)	285 – 302	29 – 30%
Cottage cheese, 1% milk fat, 2 cups unpacked	276	28%
Mozzarella, part skim, 1 ½ oz.	275	28%

Tofu, firm, with calcium, ½ cup**	204	20%
Orange juice, calcium fortified, 6 fl oz.	200 – 260	20 – 26%
Salmon, pink, canned, solids with bone, 3 oz.	181	18%
Pudding, chocolate, instant, made with 2% milk, ½ cup	153	15%
Tofu, soft, with calcium, ½ cup**	138	14%
Breakfast drink, orange flavor, powder prepared with water, 8 fl oz.	133	13%
Frozen yogurt, vanilla, soft serve, ½ cup	103	10%
Ready to eat cereal, calcium fortified, 1 cup	100 – 1000	10 – 100%
Turnip greens, boiled, ½ cup	99	10%
Kale, raw, 1 cup	90	9%
Kale, cooked, 1 cup	94	9%

Ice cream, vanilla, ½ cup	85	8.5%
Soy beverage, calcium fortified, 8 fl oz.	80 – 500	8 – 50%
Chinese cabbage, raw, 1 cup	74	7%
Tortilla, corn, ready to bake/fry, 1 medium	42	4%
Tortilla, flour, ready to bake/fry, one 6" diameter	37	4%
Sour cream, reduced fat, cultured, 2 tbsp	32	3%
Bread, white, 1 oz.	31	3%
Broccoli, raw, ½ cup	21	2%
Bread, whole wheat, 1 slice	20	2%
Cheese, cream, regular, 1 tbsp	12	1%

*Source: Heaney et al (2000).
DV=Daily Value
Calcium values are only for tofu processed with a calcium salt. Tofu processed with a non-calcium salt will not contain significant amounts of calcium.

Recommended weight-bearing exercises for children:

Bone-Building Activities (AAOS, 2003):

- Soccer
- Tennis
- Running
- Dancing
- Hiking
- Ice hockey/field hockey
- Gymnastics
- Skiing
- Baseball

- Jumping rope
- Skateboarding
- Volleyball
- In-line skating
- Basketball
- Weight-lifting
- Racquet sports
- Aerobics

Studies have shown that overtraining can cause a loss of muscle mass, resulting in a person's physique becoming too thin and unhealthy. In females, overtraining can lead to decreased estrogen production and thin bones that can easily break (AAOS, 2003).

Bicycling and swimming are not weight-bearing activities where the bones and muscles work against gravity to build bone strength and benefit bone health, but are excellent forms of exercise for overall health. If you are within a reasonable distance and the environment is safe, allowing a child to walk or bike to and from school is a great way to increase activity levels at least twice a day. Swimming is another outstanding form of exercise that renders many general health benefits — a healthy heart and increased energy levels. Playing sports at an early age is great for physical, mental, and social wellness.

Research indicates that students involved in interscholastic sports are less likely to start smoking, which is still a big problem among the youth despite all of the education given about its harmful effects (American Council on Science and Health, 2003). Many benefits of playing organized sports include learning teamwork skills, goal setting, accountability, and how to handle adversity. It is a great stress reliever for a child to "run off the frustration" in a healthy manner. Girls and boys experience higher states of psychological well-being, greater confidence and self-esteem, and a positive self-image more so than girls and boys who do not partake in sporting activities (Findlay and Bowker, 2007). There are other alternative fun, heart-pumping activities available that are mentioned in chapter two.

7. COMMUNICATING POSITIVE MESSAGES

Children go through different stages of development and experience self-doubt, insecurities, evolving perceptions of the world around them, and various forms of pressures in school both socially and academically. It is important to do everything that we can to encourage positive thinking in a child. In our society today, we see negative messages portrayed in politics, film, television, music, video games, and advertisements. We must educate children on how to best interpret, critically analyze, and overcome these negative messages, thoughts, and beliefs.

Here are some examples of negative statements given from children and positive responses given from their parents (Pantley, 1996):

"I can't do it."
Take your time and try again. I have confidence in you.

"Heather hates me."
Sounds like you're feeling rejected by Heather and that must hurt. I know you want Heather to like you. Remember that you're a very lovable kid and a terrific person, no matter what Heather, or anyone else, says or does. And, you know, she may have a problem that has nothing to do with you.

"I'm just no good in history."
You've brought up Cs before. I know you can do it again. Besides that, honey, nobody is good at everything. And look at this A in math, you've always done well with numbers!

"I'm so clumsy. I'll never learn to roller blade!"
It's tough learning something new. Remember when you first tried to ski, how hard it was? But you stuck with it, and now you're really good at skiing.

Parents should emphasize how people in our communities can help rather than hurt. For instance, we should discuss the responsibilities of both a police officer and a citizen and how mutual respect is very important for everyone in order to create a safe, thriving community.

There should also be a discussion on the specifics to why and when various forms of chemical and physical force have to be used. Another example of communicating positive messages can be highlighted in taking a yearly trip to see the physician. Visits are important and necessary from an early age and should be expressed with joy as opportunities to visit caring friends, as opposed to feeling afraid of experiencing pain.

Over the past 30 years there has been substantial research conducted to determine the effect that mass media has over the public's belief system. The effect of the mass media is very pervasive throughout the world and is one of the most significant influences on society.

Stereotypes of various professions, genders, ethnicities, and other groups of people can be heard or seen in music, newspapers, magazines, movies, on television, and on the Internet. This inaccurate information portrayed can lead to misunderstandings that become part of one's belief system resulting in potential consequences in one's dealings with other people. There is a responsibility to make it clear that the color of a person's skin, where one resides, if a person is male or female, heterosexual or homosexual, rich or poor, does not determine the character of an individual.

In addition to one's beliefs and attitudes affecting one's relationship with other people, messages can also become one's base of health. Thoughts could be healing or sickening. There is a simple, yet complex relationship between one's mind and body. Research has shown a link between physical disorders and a negative state of mind. Attitudes associated with anger, fear, depression, and greed have been demonstrated to give rise to various health conditions such as heart disease, ulcers, digestive problems, asthma, and other specific organ complications (Siegel, 1989).

For centuries, people have promoted the effect of positive emotions on a person's well being. Accumulated evidence has purported improvements in: immune system functions, adaptive coping and adjustment to acute and chronic stress, psychological resilience, the ability to recover from personal, mental, as well as physical traumas, individuals with cardiovascular disease, and the risk of stroke incidence for older people (Schneiderman et al., 2005). Much hope comes from one's perception. When one feels that there is hope, then there is a perception to live life. Positive affirmations such as "I WILL" are sources of positive empowerment.

We can also conclude from research that laughter has a positive effect on one's overall health. The act of laughing strengthens the immune system producing vitamin C, increases the blood flow to the brain, thus increasing oxygen levels similar to exercise, and helps to ease pain. In addition to an improved state of physical health, a good sense of humor can bring joy, happiness, beauty, and a peace of mind (Siegel, 1989).

Optimism and pessimism are learned behaviors and one's outlook on life can, in large part, determine one's fate. Self-talk, the messages played in a person's head about oneself and one's surroundings, determines the decisions that people make in life. Positive self-talk can help in building confidence and in handling to overcome obstacles throughout life. The power of thought turns into a self-fulfilling prophecy — either positively or negatively spoken.

Here are a few self-evident truths to be considered:

• *YOU GET WHAT YOU EXPECT.*

• *AS WE THINK, SO SHALL WE BECOME.*

• *YOUR ATTITUDE DETERMINES YOUR DESTINY.*

<u>It's all about character</u>

Watch your thoughts;
they become words.
Watch your words;
they become actions.
Watch your actions;
they become habits.
Watch your habits;
they become character.
Watch your character;
it becomes your destiny.

-Frank Outlaw

8. CREATING GOOD LIFE HABITS

Habits are a culmination of daily activities performed over and over. It takes 21 straight days to create a habit and repetitive habits, good or bad, are hard to break. Therefore, focusing carefully on creating good, positive habits is essential for success. The acquisition of skills and talents can be understood by observing developments through various stages of life development.

A toddler must learn how to walk, talk, chew, and eat food. In middle childhood, most individuals will learn to read, write, and do math. Fast forward years later into adulthood and some very advanced talents in the form of speaking multiple languages, playing musical instruments with great rhythm, excelling at different sports, cooking specialty foods, writing stories, building and designing various architectural structures, improving technology, taking on leadership roles with great effectiveness, and many other talents are exhibited. All of these feats are attainable through good habits over time. Setting goals help people see a clearer path and paint a picture that achievement is possible.

A goal is nothing more than a dream with a deadline. In order to be a high achiever, goal setting is a must. Every expert was once a beginner and taking small steps in climbing the ladder of success is the key to attaining goals. Goals are 50% more likely to be achieved when written down on paper than goals thought or spoken about (Anderson, 2006). Adults that sit down with children and help them chart out a course for achieving their goals greatly aid in those accomplishments.

The analogy of getting into a car and driving 5 miles, 50 miles, or 500 miles away is a goal. Drivers know that they will arrive at their destination. They have their course either mapped out in their head, on paper in the form of directions, or programmed into their global positioning system. There may be obstacles along the way in the form of traffic delays or detours, but eventually, their destination is achieved.

The same principle applies for any short or long-term goals. One must have a clear idea where she/he intends to go, wants to end up, and the path to take to get there. It is necessary to make these goals clear, specific, and attainable. Challenging the goal seeker, but being realistic, allows the individual to maintain a sense of confidence in the face of difficulty and keeps the process moving forward. Dreaming is good, but be aware that lofty short-term goals can be a recipe for failure.

A personal contract can be helpful in many cases for a child. Involving a rewards system for achieving short-term goals along the way can help a child remain on track if she/he has a difficult time committing to a goal. The reward can be a certificate given, a privilege granted, or a showcase of her/his work. Goal setting can include any area of life including personal relationships with family, friends and/or classmates, self-confidence, obtaining good grades, mastering a particular skill, being part of a team, being healthy, helping others, making career choices, and growing spiritually.

What if the goal to be achieved is unclear?

After working with many young people in different capacities, I have found the following practical method for finding one's desire and turning it into a focal point for goal setting to be highly successful.

- Have a brainstorm session and decide on what your goal is by making two categories: likes and dislikes and writing down everything and anything that you enjoy doing in one column and what you don't enjoy doing in the other column.

- Disregard the "dislikes" category focusing on the "likes" category.

- Branch the "likes" column into two categories: realistic and unrealistic based on current skill levels, opportunities for growth, and long-term desires and give number values (0-5) for how attainable the desire is (0 = very unrealistic 5 = very realistic).

- Disregard the "unrealistic" category and focus on the "realistic" category, those with scores of 3 or better. These remaining points provide a basis for achieving goals.

Recommended tips to help a child set goals:

- Write down your ideal life and map out from start to finish how you will get there. At various time intervals, evaluate where you are and continue towards your ultimate goal(s). You may have to make minor adjustments, re-focus, or make major overhauls, but no matter what — you are still on course to achieve your goal.

- Write down the big picture first and then work backwards mapping out a course to success from long-term to shorter-term goals.

- Set weekly, monthly, and yearly goals.

Yearly goals: **EXAMPLES**

- Make a sports team.
- Build a trusting relationship with my parents.
- Gain the respect of my peers.
- Obtain good grades at school to get into the college of my choice.
- Play an instrument very well.

Monthly goals: **EXAMPLES**

- Put on one pound of muscle and increase speed/ endurance.
- Bring home good grades and give thanks for what has been given to me.
- Take on leadership roles at school to make a difference.
- Obtain honor roll status.
- Play a song really well on a musical instrument.

Weekly goals: **EXAMPLES**

- Practice the sport 5 days a week.
- Do at least one chore a day without my parents reminding me.
- Treat others with respect by complimenting, rather than criticizing them.
- Stay organized and complete all homework assignments.
- Get proper instruction and practice an instrument and song consistently 1-2 hours each day.

The daily practice of implementing goals is fundamental to achieving success for any endeavor in life. In *Think And Grow Rich*, Napoleon Hill speaks about the importance of goal setting and that when one writes down a goal, one feels committed and has made up her/his mind; this is one's "definite major purpose." The desire becomes intensified and one becomes driven to achieve the goal set forth (Hill, 1937). Whether we realize it or not, everyone has goals, but some are more potentially life-transforming than others. One must set goals that are inspiring and allow for growth and expansion in life.

"Learning how to set and achieve a goal is perhaps the single most important thing your child can learn to prepare for school, adulthood, and for future employment. The more adept your child is at understanding this important life skill, the more options he or she will have throughout their life!"

- Gary Ryan Blair
(President of The GoalsGuy Learning Systems)

9. GETTING A CHILD MOTIVATED AND STRIVING TO ALWAYS DO ONE'S BEST

Often times, parents are in disbelief when their child underachieves at school. They can't understand why "out of nowhere" the grades suddenly drop or the desire to perform well has dissipated. There could be a myriad of explanations for why a child lacks motivation in specific areas of life including a very high level of difficulty in the subject matter, a low level of interest, a boring or mean teacher, unpopular among peers, a feeling of rejection, a feeling of boredom, unchallenging academic material, etc.

Each child possesses her/his own unique motivations. What one child finds to be motivating in school achievement, another discovers in musical accomplishment and yet another realizes in community contributions. It is important to help bring forth the "spark of life" in all children, rather than place the blame on someone for "stripping away the desire."

As a public school teacher, I have formulated specific strategies for helping children get motivated to achieve at school. An emphasis on academics is multi-layered and has many implications. In addition to the acquisition of skills and knowledge gained with consistent academic performance, self-confidence and self-value continue to grow. It is important to realize that social and emotional problems are not the cause of academic frustration and failure, but rather the consequence (NCLD, 2009).

Below are the successful strategies that I have found very useful in helping children gain the motivation to learn and achieve to the best of their abilities. Specific examples are provided that I have personally used and have served to be successful in my practice as an educator. These tips can also be utilized at various times at home.

- *Expose a child to new things.*
  - When children see something new or different, this piques their curiosity and increases their motivation to learn.
  - Presenting something already learned in a new way can increase interest levels.

- *Foster a child's interest in the classroom.*
  - The child brings in an extra credit assignment on something interesting and related to the topic and presents it to the class.
  - Have available resources for the student to explore a topic of interest further.
  - Take children on a virtual or real field trip to learn more.
  - If it is a potentially boring topic and/or a difficult concept to grasp, use at least 3 completely different methods of instruction to teach the same concept.

- *Use short-term rewards as an incentive for achievement.*
  - Offer a game day if homework is complete.
  - Play a game with the students during or after school.
  - Credit a child effort points for improvement.
  - Recognize children in different school related areas: character, participation, highest test scores, highest grade point average, most improved, etc.

- *Make connections to real-life applications.*
  - Ask questions applicable such as:
    "How does this affect you?"
    "What would happen without this?"
    "How has this shaped society?"
    "What would you do in that situation?"
  - Show how the concepts influence society through helping and/or hurting directly or indirectly.

- *Use praise to encourage a child's efforts.*
  - Use positive comments:

"Good job!"
"Your hard work pays off!"
"I knew you could do it. Now you know you can do it!"
"I see great improvement. Keep going!"
"I am proud of you!"
"You are giving great effort!"
"I believe in you!"

"You can do it!"

"I care about you."

"You are very special."

"You can talk to me anytime about anything."

"I am here to listen and help whenever you need me."

- Avoid negative comments:

"Can't you be more like your brother/sister?"

"If you weren't so lazy, you would do better."

"Do your homework, otherwise you will be punished."

"This may be too difficult for you to understand."

"You shouldn't…"

"You can't…"

"Don't…"

- *Ask for the child to teach you about the topic.*
  - You can ask, "What did you learn today at school? Can you please explain that concept for me?"
  - Children can teach not only verbally, but also through other authentic expressions such as art, music, poetry, acting, and/or writing.

- *Turn a "boring/challenging concept" into a game or an activity.*
  - Create a song or a skit to learn the material.
  - Research the topic and then have a court case/debate.
  - Work in groups with friends to design a game or an activity.

- *Involve a child in the decision-making of the learning process.*
  - Granting requests on what they would like to learn specifically within the curriculum.
  - Involve them in school-related activities and functions throughout the year: lunch menu choices, spirit days, dances, clubs, and other activities.

- *Discuss importance of a topic and how it relates to a child's interests.*

- Emphasize the importance to have an appreciation for all things in life. Show how all things are interrelated in this world.
- Each topic is unique and has its place in the world. My favorite line is, "Science is everything…from the air you breathe…to the bus that brought you to school…to the sound waves hitting your ear drums and the oxygen molecules entering your body, etc. etc."

- *Encourage visualization of a topic.*
  - Connect everyday technology to mathematical and scientific concepts.
  - Use hands on, interactive multi-media to generate intrigue.
  - Design a short story using analogies to describe concepts.
  - Create a mini-movie demonstrating concepts.
  - Illustrate concepts through a poster presentation or a comic strip.

- *Challenge a child.*
  - A talented and gifted child who is not challenged may become disinterested and channel energies in a wasteful manner.
  - Provide a child with additional resources to the curriculum.
  - Hold the standards high and allow a child to receive extra credit for school assignments that interest her/him.
  - Allow freedom to express creativity and show off skills.
  - Recognize any contributing information that a child brings to class and allow her/him to share with everyone (if so desired).

Many of the most successful people in the world have been told at one point or another in their lives that they were not smart enough to achieve what they desired or that the competition was too fierce. Each day we make choices on what messages we process and internalize from our surroundings as a part of our self-worth and value. Inner conversations have a powerful impact on one's emotional well-being and motivation to succeed. A person can accomplish many great feats with good, positive daily habits. Successful people speak in the affirmative, assenting the word "YES!" each day.

Truly successful people always work to the best of their ability and look for reasons to achieve versus excuses that something or someone is preventing them from accomplishing their goals. These people do not blame their past histories, parents, teachers, co-workers, bosses, and/or government for any failure to get ahead in life. They live by the motto, "If it's to be, it's up to me!" The efforts put forth determine a person's progress and gains in life. With great persistence, one will be amazed at what one can achieve.

The views on success from some of the top motivational speakers and authors can be summarized into eight success secrets. These ideas were taken from interviews with 15 of the nation's top motivational speakers and authors, including motivational speaker Brian Tracy, authors Les Brown and Dr. Wayne Dyer, sales motivator Mike Ferry, seminar leader Patricia Fripp, and *Chicken Soup* authors Jack Canfield and Mark Victor Hansen.

These "secrets" highlight the tools that successful people utilize to help them achieve their dreams and keep them motivated throughout the process. It is invaluable for children to understand different belief systems that co-exist, levels of commitment necessary for achievement, and positive attitudes displayed in life and integrate these ways of thinking into their own belief systems so they are able to succeed at anything they put their mind to (Jeffreys, 1996).

*8 SUCCESS SECRETS FROM MOTIVATIONAL EXPERTS

1. Take 100 percent responsibility for your life.

2. Live your life "on purpose."

3. Be willing to pay the price for your dreams.

4. Stay focused.

5. Become an expert in your field.

6. Write out a plan for achieving your goals.

7. Never give up.

8. Don't delay.

*Source: Jeffreys (1996).

The message to "be your best self" is crucial for a child to understand. Children look for others' assurance or blessings for what they do in order to be accepted, to fit in, and to be cool. It is important for adults to convey that another child's opinion does not have to become another person's reality.

Wise advice never gets old. Adults have been down similar roads as those of children growing up, even though the times change with technological advances and some different social constructs. Throughout the passing of generations, individuals growing up still possess feelings of insecurity and doubt. Those in need of help will look to caring adults for safety, security, and guidance.

This support will propel a child forward to accomplish many great, unimaginable feats throughout her/his lifetime. But young people may question if their voices can be truly heard; can they make a difference so young? An example of a marvelous accomplishment is when Michael Sessions became the youngest mayor ever (at 18-years-old) in Hillsdale, Michigan, in 2005, while still attending high school (Koch, 2005). With the right motivation and guidance — anything is possible!

10. UNDERSTANDING A CRISIS

Crisis can be triggered by a specific event that takes place during the day, at school, or at home. It can be anything from an everyday event such as a homework assignment or completing a chore around the house to a major event or rejection or punishment. Young people also experience maturational crisis as they move from one developmental stage to another. Without crisis (to a certain degree), change would not be possible (Holden, 2001).

*Four questions to ask yourself when placed in a crisis situation with a child:

1. What am I feeling now?
2. What does this young person feel, need, or want?
3. How is the environment affecting the young person?
4. How do I respond?

*Source: *Therapeutic Crisis Intervention* (Holden, 2001: 12).

*During times of crisis, it is important to actively listen to a child by:

- Being respectful to the individual.
- Being sensitive to her/his facial expressions and tone of voice.
- Allowing the individual to express her/his emotions.
- Responding to the individual's feelings, as well as behavior.
- Communicating that you care and understand.
- Helping the individual resolve the issue calmly.
- Using encouraging and eliciting techniques (e.g. "I see," "I'd like to hear more," "What happened next?").

*Source: *Therapeutic Crisis Intervention* (Holden, 2001: 33-37).

Examples of reflective responses you can use with an individual in crisis:

> *"You are upset about getting a detention. I'd be upset, too. What happened?"*

"You feel upset when your friends call you names, tell me about how that made you feel."

"Here is what I hear you saying, you felt…"

Many young people are unaware of the destructive nature of their behavior and how much power they wield over others. For instance, a child may be abusing drugs to the point of death and still feel that everything is fine. Another child may steal or vandalize and only be concerned with getting caught. Many young individuals are not bothered that their actions may be hurting a family, a community, or an individual despite understanding the consequences of their actions. They often respond differently to authority in a one-on-one situation, as opposed to a big group setting.

Sometimes groups display high levels of "individual territoriality" and "strong antigroup feelings." A key factor in strengthening positive peer influence is to build cohesive groups. This is especially a challenge for youth counselors who work with delinquent children. One of the best ways to build cooperation and unity is to provide opportunities for the group to succeed. In some residential communities, groups are given responsibilities such as cooking for others, cleaning up the environment, painting the classroom, etc. When group members see a result from their efforts, they often feel deep satisfaction and accomplishment, which improves group morale (Vorath and Brendtro, 1985).

All behavior has meaning and reflects the needs of a child. Many children react with aggression out of frustration, a loss of control to a situation, to intimidate someone, or to manipulate the situation. To get to the root of the concern, we must identify a young person's needs by asking the following questions (Holden, 2001: 19):

1. Why did this happen today, but not yesterday?
2. Is this typical behavior for this young person?
3. Is the young person expressing a need?
4. Is this normal for a young person of this age?
5. Does this behavior reflect a family or cultural belief?

In order for adults to be highly effective in helping young people control their emotions, adults have to be able to control their own feelings in a crisis situation. It is easy to get upset and act impulsively or react with criticism, sarcasm, and blame an individual, but that may very well aggravate the situation and intensify a young person's anger. Unless the individual is a danger for either herself/himself or others, avoid making physical contact with an angry, potentially violent person.

*To de-escalate a crisis, one can apply what I like to call the "SAVE ME!" technique in helping an individual recover from a crisis.

> **S**   **Speak** respectfully with conviction and control making clear requests.
> **A**   **Actively** listen to the individual.
> **V**   **Vacate** stressors from the environment (e.g. people, weapons, objects, etc.).
> **E**   **Establish** conversation by using your relationship.
> **M**   **Make** room for the individual to cool down.
> **E**   **Exit** the area giving time for the individual to respond to requests.
> **!**

*Adapted from *Therapeutic Crisis Intervention* (Holden, 2001).

Throughout this book, preventive strategies and first level intervention solutions are proposed for a wide variety of issues relating to youth. However, there are times when crisis occurs and it is important to assess the situation properly in order to identify the most appropriate therapeutic intervention strategy for a child.

> **"When the power of love overcomes the love of power,
> the world will know peace."**
>
> **- SRI CHINMOY GHOSE
> (spiritual teacher and philosopher)**

Chapter II

A Super Health Program For Today's Youth

"It becomes clear that the sort of person the prisoner became was the result of an inner decision, and not the result of camp influences alone. Fundamentally, therefore, any man can, even under such circumstances, decide what shall become of him — mentally and spiritually."

-VIKTOR FRANKL
(neurologist, psychiatrist, Holocaust survivor)

According to the World Health Organization (WHO), health is defined as "the state of complete physical, mental, and social well-being, and not merely the absence of disease or infirmity." This chapter focuses on providing a super health program that builds key components of a child's health and helps develop good habits for the future.

Growing boys and girls are in the midst of great physical and emotional changes. This period of changing hormones, body growth, and development is one of the best times of their life (believe it or not). Appearance is of the utmost importance for them, as the eyes of potentially hundreds of other spectators will see them each day. A child's days are often filled with ups and downs. Daily pressures abound from parents, teachers, coaches, friends, peers, and other school and home-based responsibilities.

How can young people seemingly balance everything out in their life? A good thing is that age is on their side and that energy arrives in abundant supplies. A child's metabolism is quite active always chewing, digesting, and spitting out energy throughout the day and the potential to utilize that raw energy is a great asset.

Inactivity is a culprit affecting so many young people, especially with today's constant boom in technology. Yes, kids need to have fun and enjoy themselves, but there are active, healthy ways to achieve this excitement. Learning to make choices in terms of how kids spend their time determines the path that they follow in their lives. How much time they dedicate towards studies, paying attention in class, what they eat each day and when, and how and in what manner to exercise are skills that must be taught, put into practice, and repeated daily.

Setting the priorities straight for a child:

1. FAMILY
2. HEALTHY EATING
3. ACADEMICS
4. EXERCISE
5. SOCIAL & LEISURELY ACTIVITIES

1. LIFESTYLE TIPS

Get a child on the road to **SUPER HEALTH!**

A good hygiene, proper eating habits, and regular exercise begin at an early age. Developing these great habits early on in a child's life will help them to see health, good nutrition, and physical activity as a regular part of everyday life that can be fun. It is a great stress release and outlet to liberate one's energy in a positive manner. The unique talents possessed by a child should be fostered early on in life. Teaching a high level of self-discipline helps to instill a sense of pride that carries over to other areas of a child's life. On the same token, encouraging children to try something new that they are interested in, but may not excel at, can help steer them towards approaching a challenge head on, rather than developing avoidance for trying new things.

Some of the greatest athletes of all time were unable to find great success at a young age, but worked very hard to break through to where they wanted to be. Children must be reminded an important message when they say they can't do it and that is "EVERY EXPERT WAS ONCE A BEGINNER!" One of the greatest basketball players in history, Michael Jordan, was cut from his high school varsity basketball team as a sophomore. He had a choice to make at 15-years-old. Give up and say, "I'm just not as good as the other guys," or pick his head up high and work to be the best that he could be.

We realize what choice in life he made. He viewed his "failure" as an opportunity to rise above and conquer the odds. That perceived failure back then was enough to spur him to greater achievements in his life.

PARENT TIP:

#1- YOU are the greatest influence in your children's lives. Support and encourage them to be THEIR best (not having to be THE best). Encourage them to eat well, exercise, work hard at school and at home, and treat others with kindness and respect. Your steady and consistent support in these avenues will become a strong part of their values.

#2- From an early age, teach a child proper hygiene in using the bathroom and washing hands. Proper manners at the dinner table are important for later meals in life with peers and business associates. Making a good first impression will be very important in developing relationships.

1.Developing sound, healthy eating habits	It is easy to have a sweet tooth and eat junk food and candy. It is also possible to get numerous cavities and put on added weight. Good strict eating habits as a child will carry into adult life. Bring lunch to school and avoid vending machines. Possibilities for success are endless when an individual incorporates good lifestyle habits early.
2. Too much technology	Habits, habits, habits! Homework is (TV, computers, cell phones, #1. Physical activity is #2. Then, a video games, music players, etc.) "tech time" reward shall be granted. Limit this time to 1 or 2 hours a night depending upon the situation. With this consistency, much success will be obtained throughout all areas of a child's life.
3. Feeling good about oneself	Always a concern, right? Finding the right clothes to wear on a daily basis and having a nice body image are issues, with most adolescents. Incorporating the "SUPER HEALTH" tips in this chapter will allow a child to feel good about herself/himself, which will ultimately translate into life long success. Children have to be

taught that inner beauty is #1 — not physical appearance.

4. Raging hormones	Puberty is a very exciting, scary, energetic, depressing, and happy time of life. Children grow physically and mentally each day. Their world is changing and it may feel chaotic. If they follow the proposed tips, they will become stronger both physically and mentally with an increased stability in their lives and will possess the courage to stand up to adversity during the most challenging times.

2. HEALTHY FOODS AND DRINKS

MYTH: Children with weight control issues should be put on specific reduced calorie diets.

FACT: Kids need to eat a healthy, varied diet to help them grow and develop — consuming a plentiful amount of daily calories.

RECOMMENDED DAILY CALORIC INTAKE (RDCI)

Caloric levels depend on age, gender, and physical activity. The figures are derived from the formulas EER (Estimated Energy Requirement) by The Institute Of Medicine for median height and weight to keep a BMI (Body Mass Index) of 21.5 for adult females, and 22.5 for adult males. For children and adolescents, more calories are needed at older ages. For adults, fewer calories are needed at older ages.

Activity Levels and RDCI (in calories)				
	Age (years)	Sedentary	Moderately Active	Active
Child	2-3	1,000	1,000-1,400	1,000-1,400
Female	4-8	1,200	1,400-1,600	1,400-1,800
	9-13	1,600	1,600-2,000	1,800-2,200
	14-18	1,800	2,000	2,400
	19-30	2,000	2,000-2,200	2,400
	31-50	1,800	2,000	2,200
	51+	1,600	1,800	2,000-2,200
Male	4-8	1,400	1,400-1,600	1,600-2,000
	9-13	1,800	1,800-2,200	2,000-2,600
	14-18	2,200	2,400-2,800	2,800-3,200
	19-30	2,400	2,600-2,800	3,000
	31-50	2,200	2,400-2,600	2,800-3,000
	51+	2,000	2,200-2,400	2,400-2,800

Some things never change!

Children need to eat their fruits and vegetables as experts have said for years. It is best for the human body to consume naturally grown products such as pesticide-free fruits and vegetables, hormone-free meat products, organic eggs, and wild, not farm raised fish to name a few. The USDA organic standards are the strictest food production standards in the world. Certified organic farms are required to follow the USDA's National Organic Standards and are regularly inspected by an independent third party (National Organic Program, 2009).

According to the National Cancer Institute (2004), scientists reported that at least 80% of cancer cases are caused by environmental factors such as agents in the water and air as well as lifestyle factors such as smoking, drinking, and diet. Exposure to pesticides and toxic chemicals at a young age can cause detrimental effects on development and later in life. The nervous, reproductive, and endocrine systems can be permanently affected by exposure to toxic substances in-utero or throughout early childhood that, at the same level, would not cause considerable harm to adults. The brain and endocrine system are highly sensitive. It is vital to minimize pesticide exposure to babies and young children in order to increase the odds for a healthy development (Protecting Children from Pesticides, 2002).

The U.S. Department of Agriculture and the Food and Drug Administration conducted studies from 2000-2007 studying 47 popular fruits and vegetables and acquired results based on an analysis of 87,000 tests for pesticides on these foods. People can lower their pesticide exposure by nearly 80% if they avoid the top 12 most contaminated fruits and vegetables and consume the least contaminated ones on the chart (Environmental Working Group, 2009).

*The Full List: 47 Fruits & Vegetables

RANK   FRUIT OR VEGETABLE   SCORE

RANK	FRUIT OR VEGETABLE	SCORE
1 (worst)	Peach	100 (highest pesticide load)
2	Apple	93
3	Sweet Bell Pepper	83
4	Celery	82
5	Nectarine	81
6	Strawberries	80
7	Cherries	73
8	Kale	69
9	Lettuce	67
10	Grapes - Imported	66
11	Carrot	63
12	Pear	63
13	Collard Greens	60
14	Spinach	58
15	Potato	56
16	Green Beans	53
17	Summer Squash	53

18	Pepper	51
19	Cucumber	50
20	Raspberries	46
21	Grapes - Domestic	44
22	Plum	44
23	Orange	44
24	Cauliflower	39
25	Tangerine	37
26	Mushrooms	36
27	Banana	34
28	Winter Squash	34
29	Cantaloupe	33
30	Cranberries	33
31	Honeydew Melon	30
32	Grapefruit	29
33	Sweet Potato	29
34	Tomato	29
35	Broccoli	28
36	Watermelon	26
37	Papaya	20
38	Eggplant	20
39	Cabbage	17
40	Kiwi	13
41	Sweet Peas - Frozen	10
42	Asparagus	10
43	Mango	9
44	Pineapple	7
45	Sweet Corn - Frozen	2
46	Avocado	1
47 (best)	Onion	1 (lowest pesticide load)

*Source: Environmental Working Group (2009). For more information on the methodology behind the study, visit http://www.foodnews.org/methodology.php.

Bones and muscles are consistently growing and getting stronger. They are starving for those "building blocks" that will create a lean, keen, igniting machine!

Top picks include:

- Chicken,
- Eggs,
- Lean ground beef,
- Nuts,
- Chili,
- Beans,
- Turkey.

Foods high in calcium will promote stronger bones and optimal muscle function.

- Low-fat cheese,
- Low-fat yogurt,
- Low-fat milk,
- Additional low-fat dairy products.

Children who are lactose-intolerant should continue eating plenty of fruits and vegetables. Eating produce helps reduce the excretion of calcium.

Eat plenty of carbohydrates! Sugar is what is needed!

What are the right kinds of sugar welcomed by the body?

- Whole wheat pasta,
- Whole wheat bagels,
- Oatmeal,
- Whole-grain cereals (e.g. Total, Cheerios, Grapenuts, Kashi Go-Lean),
- Two salads a week (containing chicken or a fish (tuna or salmon), spinach, celery, leafy veggies, olives, cucumbers, olive oil, and vinegar).

Breakfast foods to spark the day:

- Whole-grain cereal with fresh fruit (strawberries, bananas, pineapples),
- 2-3 egg whites with toast (spray butter) and orange juice,

- Whole-grain toast with peanut butter and jam,
- Smoothies (blend fresh or frozen fruits with low-fat yogurt).

Fantastic flavorful foods to have during lunch time:

- Turkey breast on rye, apple, yogurt,
- Plenty of fruits (bananas, apples, pears, oranges, grapefruits, berries, etc.).

At home or weekend foods:

- Fish (salmon, swordfish),
- More fruits,
- Choose salad bars instead of ice cream parlors (regularly speaking).

PARENT TIP:

#1- Keep desired foods of consumption in your cabinet, fridge, and freezer at all times.

#2- Cook with less fat: bake, broil, roast, poach foods.

#3- Moderation is the key! Once a week, treat your children to their favorite meal.

Drinks

Most importantly:

**STAY HYDRATED! Water is the #1 recommended liquid fuel of choice. If possible during the school day, a child should carry a 16 oz. water bottle to class and fill it up 4-5 times throughout the day. Another possibility is to leave a water bottle in a locker and in between classes, take a stop to get a drink.

Get the blender or juicer out because it is time for a healthy concoction!

FRUIT OR VEGETABLE SMOOTHIES:

Play around with a variety of mixes. Add oranges, grapefruits, apples, kiwi, strawberries, bananas, blueberries, carrots, cucumbers, etc. — whatever a child enjoys for fresh fruits or vegetables. Children will receive an excellent source of vitamins and minerals. For additional protein and calcium, add some low-fat yogurt.

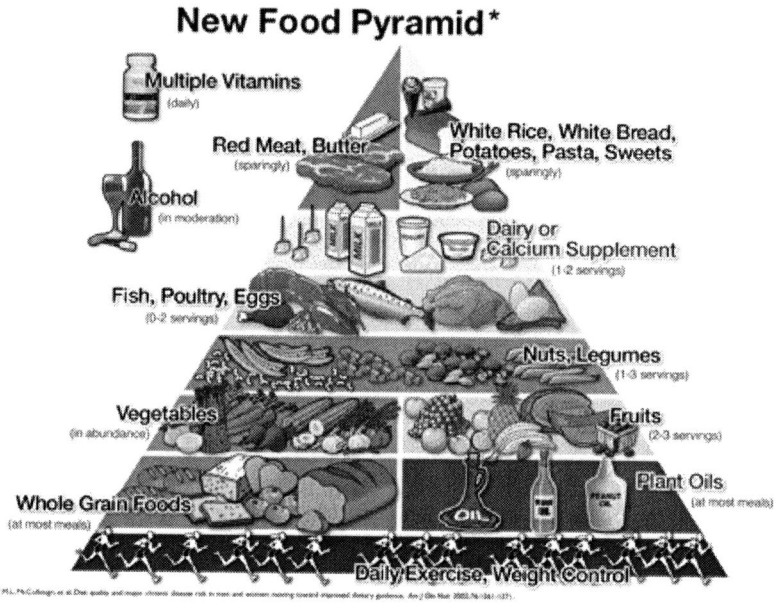

Source: Food Pyramid taken from www.richerlives.com.au.

3.   FOODS TO AVOID

Eating Junk Food

MYTH: It doesn't matter what children eat. They are young and will burn it off in no time.

FACT: Childhood obesity is four times higher now than it was 20 years ago. Life expectancy of this generation of kids is predicted to be lower than their parents.

The media fails to have it in their best interest to promote the concept of health for a child. Television viewing is a big risk factor for childhood obesity in today's day and age. Children watching television for prolonged periods are exposed to heavily advertised junk food products. On top of this notion, they have easy access to consume large quantities of junk food while they watch television.

Many children are rewarded with television for good behavior. This sedentary lifestyle is reinforced and becomes a daily habit. Children are receiving conflicting messages from many sources. Commercials and various advertisements entice young children to consume high carb/high fat foods and sway them into believing that they are good for them. Parents are then put in a precarious position as the food police and children's view of healthy food may become tainted. A behavior modification should be put into place, but who will be responsible for the education?

In the school systems, the plan is to promote healthy foods for children, but at what cost? The shelf life of fresh fruits and vegetables is shorter than frozen or canned items, making it difficult to buy in bulk and receive a discounted rate. Visiting a wide variety of schools throughout Connecticut and Southern California, I noticed that most of what is still being served in the cafeteria during lunch is high sugar, fatty, processed foods. During cafeteria duty, I would walk around and observe the food that students were eating and I would see the all-popular food swaps at lunch take place where a child would trade away her/his chicken sandwich for something less nutritious like cookies or ice cream.

In this burgeoning crisis of childhood obesity, Americans want healthier children, but at what price? We've drawn our weapons against the enemy, vending machines. A study by the Center for Science in the Public Interest (CSPI) found that of 9,723 school vending machine slots surveyed, 70% of vending machine slots held soft drinks with sugar, 42% held candy, and 5 % offered milk (less than half of those being reduced fat) (Crute, 2005). There has been much debate about whether to eliminate vending machines entirely or to replace the calorie-rich foods with something more nutritious.

Studies show that many taxpayers agree with investing in healthy foods being housed in vending machines and having a nutrition curriculum added to schools, but over half of these people were not willing to provide an extra $100 per year in taxes to support such reforms for thwarting the childhood obesity crisis. Many school administrators feel that the answer is to improve children's health and contribute to school expenses, simultaneously (Crute, 2005).

There are a growing number of schools across the nation offering healthier food choices in the cafeteria. Their strategy is to make a healthy choice a happy one for the students. As it pertains to cafeteria food, a growing number of districts across the country are making changes to the school menu and adding options of a salad bar. The institution of salad bars in various schools allows students to make their own choices for lunch, as opposed to accepting "what's on the menu." Fruit smoothies are becoming more available offering different palatable flavors such as cherry, green apple, and blue raspberry. These contain 100 % natural fruit juice (except blue raspberry — which contains 50 % natural fruit juice).

Classroom parties have changed from candy, cookies, and cupcakes to feature vegetables and dip, fruit kabobs, and cheese and crackers. School nurses are conducting "regular snack patrols" and would "catch" children eating healthy. As the school year progressed, it was noticed that more and more students would bring in healthier choices for lunch and less junk food.

Some school districts around the nation have begun farm-to-school programs that rely on local growers to supply a good stock of the cafeteria food that is fresh and nutritious for breakfast and lunch. To learn more about farm-to-school programs and see which states are participating in these programs, visit www.farmtoschool.org.

Benefits to eating happy and healthy:

Children….

- ✓ Will have more energy to do all that they want and need to do throughout the day.

- ✓ Will have a more regulated and stable mood.

- ✓ Will have blood sugar levels that remain balanced so they can concentrate at school.

- ✓ Will begin to actually see that what is "good for you" is tasty and will develop a habit for lifelong healthy eating.

Here are some TASTY DELIGHTS that parents can provide their children as healthy alternatives that are yummy in their tummy:

1. SUNFLOWER SEEDS
   - This is a great snack containing a high-fiber content and packed with protein for a growing boy and a girl. This contains "good fat" that a body needs to help protect the heart along with vitamin E, magnesium, and selenium which are very helpful in keeping a child healthy.

2. GRANOLA BARS
   - This is a great alternative to the regular candy bar. They contain more fiber and less fat.

3. MOZZARELLA STRINGS
   - These are another good source of calcium and protein. They help build strength, especially in a child's bone development.

4. POPCORN
   - Opt for the brands that are light without all of the butter or trans fat. This movie goers favorite treat is low in fat and high in fiber.

5. VITAMIN C POPSICLES

   -These pack a punch of vitamin C and other vitamins with under 100 calories for most brands and they do not contain any fat.

6. RAISINS

   -An all-time favorite and easy to pack. High in antioxidants to help prevent damage to the cells. This is an underrated champion for a snack helping to promote healthy gums and teeth. Also, raisins contain boron, which is a trace mineral useful for bone health and in protection against vision loss.

7. CORN

   -Corn on the cob without the butter contains a wallop of fiber and has been shown to have beneficial effects on the heart and the digestive system. The heart-helping nutrients include folate, magnesium, and niacin.

8. WATER

   -Making up 70-75% of our bodies, water helps rid the body of toxins, keeps a person hydrated, and maintains muscle tone throughout the body. Drink water at frequent intervals throughout the day to achieve great results.

Keep it colorful!

❖ Topping green salads with fresh fruits and veggies of different colors is not just nutritious, but colorful, also. Children like contrasting colors and playing the color game with them is a great way to get them to "eat their fruits and veggies."

*Note: Refer to the updated Food Guide Pyramid for specific recommended daily allowances for the different food groups. Amounts vary with daily physical activity levels.

The following foods should not be given to children (which contain little or no nutritional value):

• Packaged cakes and cookies,

- Canned foods high in sodium,
- White breads and pastas with refined white flour,
- Fast food,
- Pizza,
- Ice cream,
- Candy,
- High sugar cereals,
- Whole milk,
- Cheeseburgers, hot dogs, chicken nuggets, processed meats,
- High-fat condiments and dressings,
- Toppings,
- Vending machine foods,
- Soda.

Children should maintain a healthy food intake each day to maintain a healthy body.

Note: Individuals with Celiac's Disease should avoid foods that contain gluten.

Food allergies on the rise for children

According to the Center for Disease Control and Prevention (CDC), the number of young individuals with food allergies has risen 18% over the last ten years. Studies estimate that nearly three million children have a food or digestive allergy. Experts are not sure why this is the case (Possible Causes of Food Allergies, 2008). Is it that the medical industry has become more efficient at correctly identifying allergies or could it be due to the processed foods that we largely consume?

The most common foods that contain allergens include:

- Peanuts,
- Tree nuts,
- Milk,
- Eggs,
- Soy,
- Wheat,

➤ Fish,
➤ Shellfish.

It is estimated that between 70-75% of all processed foods in U.S. grocery stores may contain ingredients from genetically engineered plants. We are unaware of the actual percent because the food manufacturers and the biotech companies are not required to notify the U.S. Food and Drug Administration (FDA) that they are bringing new genetically engineered products to the market (Possible Causes of Food Allergies, 2008).

These plant types are genetically altered to possess characteristics of the original species. These crops are genetically modified to grow faster, bear more fruit, or develop their own insecticide. Long-term safety testing of genetically engineered food has not been conducted. Although, different scientists, some within the FDA, mention the potential dangers in altering the genetic makeup of a food crop and how it can trigger unexpected food allergies, create toxins in the food, or spread antibiotic-resistant disease (Possible Causes of Food Allergies, 2008).

4.   STAYING ACTIVE

❑   Practicing and playing organized sports are outstanding types of cardiovascular exercises for a child.

❑   Training with a sports-specific program outlined by a coach develops self-discipline.

❑   If a child does not play on an organized sports team, then getting involved with intramural teams after school can help to develop social and physical skills.

❑   Enjoyable exercises for children include:

  ➢   Jogging,
  ➢   Wind sprints,
  ➢   Bike riding,
  ➢   Rollerblading,
  ➢   Skateboarding,
  ➢   Simulated rock climbing (indoors),
  ➢   Hiking,
  ➢   Swimming,
  ➢   Ice skating,
  ➢   Skiing,
  ➢   Various climbing and jumping exercises,
  ➢   Karate,
  ➢   Cardio kickboxing,
  ➢   Dancing,
  ➢   Yoga, Pilates, Tai Chi.

GET PUMPED UP!

•   Listening to music while working out is more fun and gets an individual energized and motivated. Studies have shown that individuals who work out to music have better results in terms of reduced anxiety, decreased blood pressure, reduced cancer risks, weight loss, and/or muscle gain since music keeps a person moving more and revs up the metabolism (Kreamer,

2007). There are many dance classes that incorporate different styles of music to a workout that may interest a child.

Get a child involved and enjoy the awesome benefits.

BUILD A CHILD'S FUTURE…**NOW!**

Being part of a physically active social group builds:

- Social skills,
- Teamwork,
- Patience,
- Self-discipline,
- Positive habits,
- Character for future challenges in all areas of life.

Various mind-body activities such as Tai Chi and Yoga can help increase mind and body flexibility, alertness, concentration, focus, and overall mental strength. This is a great way to carve away the stresses in one's life. If a child wants to be the best at her/his sport, practice on a consistent basis must take place. Players should listen to their coach, even if things appear unfair in the situation. There may be times (occasionally or frequently) in which athletes feel that their hard work is not being recognized and that they do not get enough playing time. There is no need for complaining. Rather, a solution needs to be drawn up and this is where a parent, teacher, older sibling, or another adult close to a child can make a difference. A child may need to work that much harder than her/his other teammates and continue to work harder. These positive efforts will certainly shine through — whether it is immediately or later on. The important message is that all good deeds never go unnoticed and unrewarded.

With technology advances occurring on a daily basis, the temptation for many children is to get the latest and greatest video game and sit down for hours trying to conquer all of its challenging levels. It is easy for a child to sit down for a long time by herself/himself or with friends and be unaware of how quickly time passes. Playing video games, text messaging on cell phones, and listening to music on the newest music player deprive a child from spending quality time moving more.

Health is undoubtedly the most important factor in one's life and keeping active is something that has become a challenge for today's generation of children, as a whole. The good news is that youth have the education and power in their hands to make smart decisions. Keep in mind that human beings are creatures of habit and repeated patterns are hard to break; therefore, getting young people on the road to super health early is paramount. Later in this book, a discussion is made about the topic of obesity and what can be done to help reverse this trend of being the fattest society in the world.

First off, schoolwork is the highest priority, followed by daily exercise. If a child has successfully completed both of those tasks, then a reward such as watching a television show, playing on the computer/video games, or talking to a friend on the telephone for a brief period of time is warranted. A child could exercise in front of the television by doing a set of pushups and situps during commercial breaks.

PARENT TIP:

#1- Have your child carry pedometers to track how many steps she/he takes. This can help a child realize the value of getting up and moving regularly. Set a goal for 10,000 steps a day (approximately 5 miles). You may be surprised at the level of pride that a child takes in doing this (if presented correctly).

#2- Be involved in your child's physical activities by making it a daily routine (e.g. throw a baseball, shoot baskets, run with them, etc.). If your schedule does not allow for that, get her/him involved with programs at a club or a YMCA/YWCA and/or encourage participation in school-related activities.

#3- Assign weekly chores for a child to do that will get her/him up and about such as mowing the lawn, vacuuming the house, gardening, taking out the garbage, etc.

It is understood that a child is required to sit in a chair for most of the day at school. During this time, there is an opportunity to control health by sitting up in a chair with good posture. This is another hard habit to break and it is noticeable in a large number of people, as they get older — appearing slouched over or having a rounded back posture.

For good posture, a child should sit with:

- Chest out,
- Spine erect,
- Shoulders back and downward away from the ears,
- Head held up high,
- Navel drawn into spine,
- Taking in regular full capacity breaths from the abdominal region (diaphragmatic breathing), as opposed to shallow chest breathing.

5.   STRENGTH TRAINING

Before doing any exercise, it is recommended to consult with your physician.

MYTH: Lifting weights will stunt a pre-teen/teen's growth.

FACT 1: There is no minimum age for beginning weight training.

FACT 2: Children need 60 minutes of moderate to vigorous physical activity every day.

FACT 3: Weight training programs are becoming mandatory at schools.

If a child is engaged in a school sport, she/he can follow the resistance-training program that a coach designs specifically to enhance performance. Young athletes can follow the given routines below and incorporate these weight-training programs into their schedule during the off-season.

KNOWING THE VOCAB!

- ➤ *FAILURE* - lifting weights to exhaustion (e.g. 10 bicep curls to exhaustion, 8 curls = 80% failure)

- ➤ *MUSCLE ENDURANCE* - increasing the ability for muscles to do what you ask them to do when you increase physical activity

- ➤ *MUSCLE STRENGTH* - a muscle's ability to exert force (e.g. pushups/situps)

- ➤ *REPETITION* - performing an exercise in a set (e.g. 10 bicep curls in a row to 70% failure = 10 repetitions of bicep curls)

- ➤ *SET* - a group of repetitions performed for a given exercise

(e.g. 10 bicep curls in a row to 70% failure = 1 set of bicep curls)

Ready, set, go, but do it RIGHT!

❖ **Elementary / Middle (Junior high school) school-aged children**

➢ *Go to 70-75% FAILURE when weight training. This means that children DO NOT lift until they are exhausted, but rather to ¾ of their maximum capacity.*

➢ *The key for their workout is HIGH REPETITIONS and CORRECT FORM.*

The goal of resistance training at this age is to build MUSCLE ENDURANCE and MUSCLE STRENGTH.

BOYS & GIRLS:

> **When:** *3 days a week*
> **Type:** *2 sets/exercise; 15 repetitions/set*

1. Pullups*
2. Pushups*
3. Dumbbell curls
4. Shoulder presses
5. Abdominal crunches*
6. Bodyweight squats
7. 50 Jumping Jacks*
8. 50 Jump rope skips*

*For these exercises, perform additional reps (90-95% failure) if possible.

❖ High school-aged children

➢ *Children will begin an advanced resistance-training program, since they are at later stages of adolescence.*

➢ *If they are on a sports team, they should consult with their coach and follow the sport-specific program that is specifically laid out for them.*

➢ *They can work out at their school gym, if there is availability.*

BOYS: 3 sets, 10-15 repetitions (85% failure or 90-95% failure with a spotter)
GIRLS: 3 sets, 12-15 repetitions (70-75% failure or 75-80% failure with a spotter)

When: *3 days a week*

➢ Stick to the basic compound movements below that recruit all of the major muscle groups.

1) Barbell bench press*
2) Seated lat row
3) Leg press (or squat*)
4) Leg extensions
5) Barbell bicep curls
6) Seated military shoulder presses
7) Lying crunches**
8) Hanging leg raises

* Perform only if there is a reliable spotter and if they can be performed with good form.
** Perform more repetitions if possible.

Rising (and falling) to the challenge!

Youth Challenge #1

• When children are able to perform 50 pushups without stopping, they can do a set of pushups where they place their feet on a chair, thus forming an inclined plane, keep their hands in the same position as done for the regular pushups, and perform as many pushups as possible.

Youth Challenge #2

- Another pushup exercise to shock the upper body and build core strength involves the assistance of a workout buddy. The individual should perform a set of regular pushups to about 80-85% failure and on the last repetition, a workout partner should stand directly over the individual and pick up her/his body and then the individual can allow the body to lower slowly and repeat this action for about 5 repetitions (maintaining the pushup position). On the final repetition here, without the help of the workout partner, the individual should perform as many pushups as possible on her/his own.

Youth Challenge #3

- Perform diamond pushups where children place their feet on the ground as they normally would for a standard pushup and place the index fingers and thumbs in a manner where they touch and form a diamond between the hands. This exercise not only works the pectoral muscle group, but also strengthens the triceps.

PARENT TIP:

#1- Provide a basic, easy to set up bench, along with a dumbbell set, for a child to work out in an area of the house or outside.

#2- Sign up for a family package at a local YMCA and attend with your child. This will help motivate her/him to follow the program consistently (and it could not hurt for a parent to get some exercise, too). In some areas of the United States, there are gyms specifically designed for youth — where the machines are ergonomically designed and age-specific for different age brackets of children.

#3- Get involved with your child's workouts initially to make sure that form for the exercises are correct by getting her/him the proper assistance needed. This stage of adolescence tends to be more impulsive and careless. Monitor a child carefully and build a consistent routine for her/him to follow.

"The best way to stay in shape is to never get out of shape."

-CAL RIPKEN, JR.
(hall of fame major league baseball player)

Chapter III
LIFESTYLE CHALLENGES TARGETING TODAY'S YOUTH

"There is no greatness where there is not simplicity, goodness, and truth."

-LEO TOLSTOY
(novelist, philosopher)

It is important to examine the factors that contribute to various health and lifestyle challenges that youth and adults can encounter beginning from childhood. Blaming others for problems in today's society and making excuses are not the answers. Each person should know her/his unique role to play in impacting another's life, especially a child's life. Adults' actions directly impacting children will ultimately come back full circle to affect the future. Effectively changing the world starts from understanding yourself.

Education for children is only as powerful as it is reinforced daily at home, in the schools, and within our communities. It is important to understand that these pillars that help build a child's persona can be places that are warm, loving, and caring, but they can also be tense, cruel, and abusive. This depends on the behaviors and actions that may be demonstrated by a child's family members, friends, classmates, teachers, fellow citizens, and mass media.

This chapter examines the different challenges that youth can face, describes the root causes for these issues, and proposes methods to best prevent or rectify a potentially problematic situation. Different problems are caused by various factors and require different solutions. Keep this point in mind as you read through this chapter when trying to help a child. With this understanding, a difference can be made, not only in the lives of young people, but in your life, also.

1. DISHONESTY

Situations will arise throughout life where a child will be faced with telling the truth or making up a lie to address a particular situation. Dishonesty includes a wide range of unacceptable behaviors including selling drugs for money, bootlegging movies and games, lying to others, cheating on school assignments, stealing, fighting, and inflicting cruelty on others. These actions are unfair to people who have been victimized whether they are family, friends, or complete strangers. Most prominently, they are unfair to the child who has performed the dishonest act.

How could it be unfair to a person who committed the act? It is important to remember that habits are difficult to break. When lying takes place at a young age and is repeated for a prolonged time, it affects all aspects of that person's life. Relationships are torn apart and families are destroyed because of lies. You may have experienced hardships either first hand in your family or through a friend because of lies and manipulation.

Addressing dishonest behavior, early in one's life, is the most effective way of preventing habitual or compulsive lying. Children lie for many reasons and most individuals grow up to be fine, working, respected citizens. Chronic lying can cause serious problems at home, at school, and lead to further problems into adulthood.

One's character, attitude, and values are fundamental to success down the road. As time takes its natural course, we assume that as children grow into young adults, they seek to move away from home and find a nice place of their own to live that is safe and comfortable — where they can enjoy a peaceful life. In order to find a nice place to take residence, have a job that is enjoyable and resonates with your being, foster relationships, and possess a strong mind and body, all parts need to be working in harmony and children need to be taught what is required for reaching long-term success.

The root of unhappiness in life does not stem from failing to achieve something, but rather from being dishonest with oneself and others. Many people escape reality and turn to alcohol and drugs when they could not express truth in their own lives, which unfortunately hinder people from solving their problems and moving forward. Most importantly, making conscious decisions not to tell the truth can scar one's inner being and dim a bright light that would be shining, otherwise.

We are all unique in our own way and we have the right to feel lost, confused, down, and out of it at times, but it must be understood that everyone in the world experiences difficulties and life tragedies to some degree. Everyone has choices to make about the kind of person that they want to be and how they would like to be viewed and treated by others.

Keeping a positive outlook on life even when it seems that nothing is going right may seem nearly impossible at times. Children learn behaviors at home and witness first-hand examples of truth and lies. Even if a child grows up in a tough neighborhood where violence and stealing are equated with survival, it is the family that should teach a child that there are alternative options to choose from in order to have a good life — one of them is asking for help to find the way. The message that "things turn around for good people and miracles happen," is a powerful "truthism."

Children lie to parents and teachers about doing their homework, cheating on tests, and stealing from stores because they know the truth will make adults angry and disappoint them. Can you believe that in some areas of the world such as the Middle East, stealing could render some serious, irreversible consequences where the legal system is really strict and order for the removal of a hand or another body part?

What is the big deal with lying?

"But it's only lying."
"Everyone does it."
"Most of the time they are just white lies."
"Kids naturally do this to impress others or to be accepted."

"It's part of growing up."
"Not telling the truth can save someone from pain."
"I had no choice, but to lie."

These statements may be justifiable in select cases, but in the circle of life, one will find that "the truth will indeed set you free." In order for children to appreciate the value of that phrase, they have to feel safe in confiding their feelings openly and honestly with adults and that they are being listened to, understood, and valued. To feel whole within oneself is very important and is an ongoing process that is built early on at the familial level.

Lying hasn't received much attention as a big problem severely affecting children, but it has taken on acclaim by being popularized as "truthiness" (on the Comedy Central television channel — the *Colbert Report*). The American Dialect Society voted "truthiness" as one of its past "Words of the Year" and refers to "the quality of preferring concepts or facts one wishes to be true, rather than concepts or facts known to be true" (Mauro, 2007). How serious is it to display "truthiness" versus blatant lying? Can a distinction be made between the two?

Young children are often expected to display "truthiness" because parents don't expect them to understand the implications of their actions. While on the other hand, as children get older and there is a lack of truth-telling, this is interpreted as blatant lying because they realize the consequences of their actions. Keep in mind that children with various mental disorders and/or learning disabilities may not realize the cause and effect relationships to their actions as well as their peers understand it. Therefore, their versions of truth may actually be what they really thought it to be or wish it to be. Those having trouble with language processing may have had difficulties in understanding what was asked or expected of them. Also, individuals with sensory perception problems may not have a clear awareness of their environment and misinterpret their surroundings (Mauro, 2007).

Why do children not tell the truth?

Children lie for different reasons at different ages. Here are some of the most common reasons (Mauro, 2007):

- They don't want to disappoint others and instead tell people what will make them happy.
- They don't want to be punished.
- They want to avoid doing something unpleasant.
- They are covering up more serious problems (i.e. substance abuse, alcohol, gambling, learning disabilities, etc.).
- They want to impress others.
- They want to be accepted (fear of rejection).
- They wish for something to be that way.
- They really don't know what is true.
- They seek attention from others.
- They are telling what they truly believe to be the truth.
- They don't feel safe and secure enough to tell the truth.
- They have a poor self-esteem and feel bad or embarrassed about their current situation.
- They can't think calmly and feel highly stressed.
- They are impulsive and/or compulsive and react abruptly.
- They don't understand the difference between fantasy and reality.

BEING PROACTIVE!

How can adults promote a child's willingness to tell the truth?

- First and foremost, be the best example of truth in all that you do in your life and model honest behavior.

- Teach the value of honesty at home and at school. A discussion of being honest will help a child grow up to be an honest adult.

- Set up a safe, caring environment that promotes a child to be honest by assuming that family members tell the truth.

- Don't ever tell a child to lie or not tell the other parent something. This action will provide a confusing message to the child and can lead to chronic lying.

- Praise truth telling, especially if it was difficult for them to do so.

- Let a child know that telling the truth won't get her/him in trouble or teased by peers.

- Expect good from a child and make it clear that you trust her/him.

- Involve a child in developing rules at home and at school. Do not burden a child with too many rules and expectations.

RECOVERY!

How can we address a child who has lied?

- Be calm. Don't overreact to the situation and belabor a lie. Give a child a chance to confess a lie and explain why she/he chose to do that.

- Investigate. Try to discover underlying reasons for why a child has lied and address the issue.

- Discuss the effects of lying on others and relationships with others.

- Address the actual act of lying and not the child who lied.

- If someone in the family is displaying an undesired action that a child is modeling, address that family member privately to resolve the matter and then discuss the behavior separately with a child.

- For repeated lies, make a child responsible for her/his actions. For example, if a child hasn't done homework, rather than taking away privileges immediately, make the child accountable by getting a progress report from the teacher and then make her/him complete those missed assignments (no matter if credit for the assignment can be obtained or not). If the report is consistently good, then a child has earned back a parent's trust and learned a valuable lesson.

- Give a child the opportunity to earn back the trust broken. Forgive her/him and move forward. Do not use that action against her/him in the later future.

There are intervention programs for individuals and families available to help with more serious cases. Contacting trained professionals such as school psychologists, guidance counselors, and social workers can be helpful.

It's all about the TRUTH...the WHOLE TRUTH!

Here are some questions to discuss with a child when she/he is faced with a choice to tell the truth or lie in various situations.

- Would I be proud of the choice that I made?

- Would those who truly care about me respect that decision?

- Would I strengthen my inner being by making that choice?

- Would I help someone more by doing that?

- Would I want someone to treat me that way?

If the child answered "NO" to ANY of the above TRUTH QUESTIONS...
The action was not completely truthful.

If the child answered "YES" to ALL of the above TRUTH QUESTIONS...
Great decision made!

Being truthful is a key step in living a happy and healthy life. This book does not address the experience of disease with chronic "untruth." However, be aware that our bodies are a reservoir for our emotions, which translate into energy flow being either continuous or blocked. The experience of disease is associated with a deviation from health and being out of mind, body, and spirit balance. Self-mastery is coming to understand yourself and being truthful with yourself and the surrounding environment. Hence, balance in one's life can be achieved.

2. UNFRIENDLY COMPETITION

MLB Commissioner Bud Selig made a decision back in the 2002 All-Star game that demonstrated the ingrained nature of competition in society and how it can turn bad. When it was announced during the 11th inning that the game would be called if neither team scored, the fans erupted with boos and threw plastic cups and seat cushions onto the field. Where does this frustration stem from when it is merely a baseball game? Put simply, people like to see winners prevail.

Competition is the main message broadcast in our society. We live in a society that eats, sleeps, breathes, and motivates through competition. The time of success being defined as "reaching one's personal maximum potential" is no longer the standard. In professional sports, the season begins with the goal of "winning the championship." In entertainment, it is the awards and accolades presented to the "best this" or "best that." In education, it is the class rankings, prizes, awards, and scholarships that are given to the "best in the class." On television, it is statements like "You're going home," "You've been eliminated," and "You're not good enough for this competition," that have struck an infectious and addictive cord with millions of viewers begging for more of the same.

Competition can adversely affect the self-esteem of an individual where one would hear and think that she/he is not good enough and then decide to quit at something that was inherently pleasurable. To be chosen first at something indicates a competition for something valued, which consequently indicates that someone will be chosen last or eliminated first — deeming one a social failure. The pressure to be popular, smart, and to fit in all relate to Charles Darwin's "Survival of the Fittest" model. In some schools, there are student comparison charts displaying grades. In addition to the public embarrassment most likely felt by low-achieving students, middle or higher achieving students can lose motivation and not strive to attain their potential because they see that everything is fine as long as they are beating someone else. Effort becomes limiting, by nature, with this kind of competition.

Parental involvement is key to helping a child build healthy a self-perception and self-esteem with words of encouragement and praise, but even the best of intentions could pose the threat of unfriendly competition. Many of today's parents are obsessed with boasting their child's accomplishments for the world to know. Most have the best of intentions by doing so and lack a mean aim at other parents' children, but they are usually unaware that they are promoting competition among children. Praising the athletic, intelligent, talented, and gifted with encouragement is one thing, but separating a child from others as being "better than her/him" or ignoring and/or putting down a child for lacking success is a whole new ball game. These gestures, often times unintentional, can trigger unfriendly competition among different families of parents and children causing hurtful, personal attacks.

In the past decade, parents have announced the academic success of their child on the bumpers of their cars, "My Child is An Honor Student at…" This recognition of academic achievement was proclaimed as nothing more than a modest source of parental pride. This perception was not the view taken on by a large sector of parents and teachers. This personal pride became a heightened public issue where outraged parents were calling this an "elitist" act and chose to retaliate with their own bumper stickers saying, "My Kid Beat Up Your Honor Student" or "Your Kid May Be An Honor Student But You're Still An Idiot!" The issue here is not whether we should or should not have an honor roll system in schools. The primary concern is what children learn about the value of competition.

Is competition merely the way of the world, the nature of the beast? Is it true that life is a competition: eat or get eaten? Reading through this chapter and thinking back to your own personal experiences throughout your life, can you recall when life appeared to be such a dog eat dog world? Glorifying success, encouraging competition, and promoting one person as better than the rest — is it really all that harmful on one's self-esteem and perception on what is important in life or have we become oversensitive to it all?

As a teacher, coach, mentor, and other functional roles working with children over the years, I have seen the competitive fire sparked on various occasions. If you watch children play sports (organized or not), do you see them playing for exercise and to build their developmental skills or do they play to win? Most often, we see that when children are left to choose teams, they consider who will help carry their team to victory, rather than select a balance of different abilities to play for fun. As a former athlete at school, I have heard different philosophies from my coaches and remember some of the most reverberating exclamations:

"We are going for the big W!"
"Winning isn't everything. It's the only thing!"
"You go out there and kick some a** and win!"

As a player and a coach in sports, I have witnessed the atmosphere of youth athletics display coaches and spectators screaming at players and officials for every little mistake. Coaches would berate their players in front of their peers and pull them out of the game at a moment's notice when a mistake is made to replace them with someone "better." The action of not playing everyone on the roster and emphasizing the need to do whatever it takes "to win" is a common reinforcement given to today's youth.

How could we blame children for behaving so critically and with such belligerence considering what they have witnessed and experienced first-hand in school with the emphasis put strictly on grades and awards and in athletics as being number one and achieving victory over other teams. I have also ignited that flame with my own creative helping of competition. Have I contradicted what I am addressing as a concern for today's youth if I, myself, am promoting competition in the classroom and athletic arena?

Are there benefits in competition?

Can a child play fairly, without external rewards, winners and losers, have fun focusing on one's personal performance and still compete? Is there such a thing as "healthy competition?" Many individuals may say that this term is oxymoronic, contradicting itself and that competition, by nature, is unhealthy. Others may say that healthy competition is a synonym for cooperation and that working together for common goals is much more beneficial than working separately in competition. Educators work in an era where they teach to standards in order to mass-produce success in every educational moment and "Leave No Child Behind."

One of the strategies that have spread throughout schools is to create inclusive classrooms that mandate educators to teach all learning abilities in one classroom. The idea of promoting cooperative learning came with a reality check to this educational ideal. High-achieving students are forced to learn at the pace of lower-achieving students. When put into groups, the mix of children does not always blend and certain students pick up the slack, while others just slack off (Issues, 1995). The educational practice of inclusion and "No Child Left Behind" are noble concepts that have their benefits. On the other hand, is it truly providing a child with a meaningful cooperative experience? That shall be left for debate.

Here are some examples of what I like to call…

THE ANSWER PLEASE…

"COOP*etition* /COMP*eration* "

ADMINISTRATORS can…

- Work to GET RID of the class ranking system and traditional grading system and come up with school or region specific alternative assessments that are authentic. Many schools across America have eliminated such distinctions and honors and have seen an increase in student motivation for personal achievement.

- Develop a WIDE range of activities for all students to participate in and be successful without having to try out and experience rejection.

- Give students a CHOICE to pursue advanced level classes if they so choose knowing full well that they are given that option.

- Work to find an ALTERNATIVE means of rewarding students for their hard work, good deeds, and talents. I was part of a behavior modifications team at my school that developed a system for students to be "caught doing something good."

The student would be rewarded for acts of good citizenship, creativity displayed, acts of kindness, outstanding academic achievement, and it was unifying in its message that we are all here to help one another.

- Support educators with the TIME and RESOURCES to teach a creative, challenging curricula to children.

- Provide a PRESENTATION that clearly outlines the goals of the school/district and to involve the board of education and other outstanding figures in the process of obtaining a budget that is adequate for success to take place.

COACHES can...

- Emphasize the concept of HAVING FUN.   Encourage team members to play fairly and with respect — helping an opposing player up if she/he falls, wishing the other team well at the start of the game, and shaking hands upon completion. Congratulate the other team on a job well done, regardless of the outcome.

- Demonstrate RESPECT. Coaches being respectful to other coaches and officials set the best example for child-to-child and child-to-official interactions.

- Emphasize the concept of TEAMWORK. The old adage that there is no "I" in team is so true, but not that the team is only as strong as its weakest link.   Each person is important and has a job to do. This fosters a trusting community within a team.

- Focus on the POSITIVES. Keep a player in the game even if she/he makes a mistake, rather than reinforcing that a mistake made equals sitting on the bench. When it is time for that player to sit down, then an appropriate discussion of the situation can take place. Saying something like "You made a good attempt to run the play, but let's try it this way and see what happens," is much more constructive, than stating, "What is the matter with you? Johnny knows the play and how to run it. Why can't you?" which can destroy self-esteem, creativity, and one's concentration on the task.

- Compliment EFFORTS. Pointing out "little things" done well can go along way for one's self-esteem. When I was 13 years old, I played at a summer basketball camp and remember my instructor consistently telling me how well I boxed out for the rebound, applauding me each time I grabbed the ball. These compliments inspired me to work on my defense and led to me being named "Best Defensive Player" on the varsity basketball team during my junior and senior years of high school. Oops — external rewards, but the difference here was that I never knew about this award. It was a complete surprise!

PARENTS *can…*

- Respect the INDIVIDUALITY of a child. Treat each child with her/his unique characteristics refraining from making comparisons with siblings. Giving a child her/his own identity is very important for self-growth.

- Encourage a child to VOLUNTEER to help other children. Being a big brother/big sister and participating in mentor programs fosters cooperation, rather than competition. Acts of giving go a long way to build one's self-esteem.

- Be a positive ROLE MODEL for a child. Your child mirrors many of your actions, even the ones that you may find undesirable. Being conscientious to exhibit behaviors that you desire for your child is important for character building. Be genuinely positive and you will see positive. Our nature is based on repetitive thoughts and the thoughts that we think today are mainly what we thought yesterday. Be aware of your thoughts — they form your actions and this ultimately creates your destiny.

- Promote a child for giving her/his BEST EFFORTS. Making a comparison with others does not recognize the value of an individual. State specific strengths that a child displays and also mention constructive feedback complimented by a tangible solution. An example in sports can be: "Nice swing today. You weren't catching any breaks out there, but you were swinging well and made good contact. Keep it up. Just put a little more "oomph" into it. Stay confident and you will see that it will definitely come together in time. Nice job!"

- Focus on EFFORTS, NOT OUTCOMES. An example in academics can be: "I see that you are trying your best. Next quarter, we'll keep working hard and improve to be the best that we can be." Using the word "WE" makes a child feel that you are involved and are right there every step of the way and that life is not a lonely journey. If efforts are below standard, you can ask a child which study strategies are being used and next quarter to try something else to see what works best and mention, "Life is a learning experience and that even I am still learning new ways to improve. Learning never ends."

Competition should not be evaluated simply as good or bad, but rather analyzed in its application. The focus to be number one, succeeding at someone else's failure, participating in activities that promote unfriendly competition, and losing perspective of striving to be the best that one can be are being done quite often and become downright destructive. Think for a moment at the goals that schools have for children — to become respectful citizens, high academic achievers, tolerant individuals, caring and loving people, and develop healthy self-esteems.

In a competitive society, as is particularly evident in American culture, these goals that we have for children conflict with the messages given that it isn't good enough to simply do one's best; rather, one must triumph over others. The victor and the defeated both become intertwined in a psychological vicious circle where self-worth is determined through external sources. The more a victor competes, the further she/he has to continue to make herself/himself feel good. The "defeated" individual's self-esteem and confidence become rattled and if the experience is prolonged and repeated, feelings of anger and aggression may emerge.

Like anything in the world, a blend of yin and yang, hot and cold, light and dark, fast and slow, relaxed and excited, the two belong together — competition AND cooperation. The answer in their success lies in how they are combined.

3.   GAMBLING

It appears that many young people's heroes and icons have shifted from athletes and rock stars to gaming legends on the poker table. Television is cashing in big time on attracting youth to the gambling arena and this may seem like a cool thing to do for many youth and a way to strike it big, but so many who have walked in their shoes are not "playing with a full deck" any longer. They are walking around with empty pockets wishing that they could have taken it all back, if they had only listened to those who cared.

Many of our young wagers possess grandiose ideas of becoming gaming legends and making a lot of money.   Many of them want to "study" to become professional gamers. They read books, take classes, and play online in rooms preparing to play with the big boys for that "one chance to win it all" whether it be poker, Texas Hold 'em, Omaha, Black Jack, 7 Card Stud, and/or other "enticing" games. Does this sound like a worthwhile future? Whether or not this is a fad of pop culture or a hyped up media product remains to be seen. Separating fantasy from reality for a moment and observing from all perspectives lead us to the facts.

Pathologic gambling and problem gambling affect approximately 5 to 15 million Americans and are common in young people (Unwin, 2000). According to the Center for Addiction Studies at Harvard, gambling is the fastest growing teen addiction where it prevails as the most severe type of addiction among today's youth. Louisiana State University reports that individuals in juvenile detention are at about a four times greater risk to have a gambling problem as their peers. Roughly two-thirds of the youngsters in juvenile detention have openly admitted to stealing specifically to finance gambling (Youth and Gambling, 2007).

Here are the facts (Youth and Gambling, 2007):

- Some individuals quit in their pursuit for riches on the tables after playing in a few tournaments and realize that they have exhausted too much time and money. They notice other aspects of their lives that have suffered during the process.

- A staggering 96% of compulsive gamblers began gambling before the age of 14. These people remain attached to gambling for quite some time even though their family and friends around them have become adversely affected. In lieu of the problems that continue to arise, these people continue to gamble.

- Studies indicate that gambling increases when economic hardships become prevalent. Individuals that are concerned about keeping their jobs and providing the basic needs for themselves and their families are most prone to partake in gambling activities.

- Legalized gambling greatly affects the poor and disadvantaged. The National Bureau of Economic Research indicates that the poor bet a much larger share of their income than the working or middle class.

It is important to educate children about the realities of gambling at a very early age. The place where most youth learn to gamble is not out with their friends, but with their family. Enjoying some time with family at home playing cards is quite different from going out regularly to play cards for money — but the seed is planted at the familial level. This is an atmosphere that is inviting for trouble and often times, marks the beginning of a gambling problem. Many adult gamblers reported starting to seriously gamble at around 10-years-old. Casual gambling for money at any early age has the strong possibility of leading to a more serious problem down the road (Unwin, 2000).

Legalized gambling has been claimed as a way to raise taxes effectively and painlessly. Additionally, supporters propose that it will rid of illegal gambling. This justification from legalized gambling proponents does not take into account the hidden social impact that legalized gambling has on youth and adults, alike. They assume that all people will gamble anyway, so why not make it legal and the state can collect in this manner. Enticing those who normally would not gamble is what has been observed (Youth and Gambling, 2007).

In states with different numbers of games, participation rates increase steadily and sharply as the number of legal types of gambling increases. States that lack legalized gambling possess half as much social betting (35%) as compared to states with 3 legal types of games (72%). When legal types of gambling are introduced, the illegal gambling rate more than doubles from 9 to 22%. Furthermore, commercial gambling increases by 43%, from 24 to 67% (Youth and Gambling, 2007).

The National Council on Problem Gambling also reports that among young people who gamble, 50% are likely to binge drink and 75% are likely to smoke marijuana (Volkow, 2007). The media is very influential in targeting this audience and will prophesy that "gaming" (they won't dare say the word GAMBLING) actually helps build social skills, mathematical skills, problem-solving skills, self-discipline, concentration, and skills in reading mannerisms of people. This is one of the most brainwashing, preposterous messages given to deplete money and cause long-lasting problems down the road. This is NO GAME and I'll bet anyone on that (figuratively speaking)!

The warning signs for compulsive gambling (Youth and Gambling, 2007):

- Becoming more affixed with sports scores and point spreads.
- Increased knowledge of betting-related events.
- Drastic mood shifts for no apparent reason.
- Poor coping skills.
- Shift in the group of friends to gambling acquaintances.
- Appearance of sudden wealth.
- Frequent requests for money.
- Acts of stealing.
- Missing money and/or possessions in the house.
- Increased irritable, impulsive, and/or hostile behavior.
- Missing school or work.
- Seeing actual gambling merchandise around the house (books, CDs, DVDs, scratch offs, lottery tickets, etc.).

TAKING A LOOK AT THE BIG PICTURE...

Here are the consequences to the problem:

- Negative implications in relation to compulsive gambling include: loss of employment, emotional and financial despair, troubled relationships, substance abuse, crime, and even suicide.

- The social impact of gambling begins as that person's addiction, but then becomes a much more serious matter destroying the lives of individuals and families from all backgrounds.

- The more a person gambles, the more she/he wants to gamble for higher stakes with greater risks. This could cross over to other areas of a person's life, thus resulting in co-occurring addictions (i.e. alcohol and/or substance abuse).

*Source: Youth and Gambling (2007).

How can parents step in and address this issue before it becomes a problem?

Here are specific statements that can be said to a child addressing the issue:

- ➢ *"Easy come and easy go as they say with money and health if they are not valued and invested."*

- ➢ *"If something were easy in life and one could spawn millions of dollars from doing it, wouldn't you think that everyone would take part in the action?"*

- ➢ *"The number of lives that have been ruined, the number of families that have been destroyed, and the number of homeless people on the streets are unimaginable…and in large part because of gambling. All of those people wish they would have listened before, but unfortunately didn't and ruined so many lives."*

If a young adult is of age to legally gamble and wishes to go to the casino, clearly paint the picture about gambling.

WORDS OF WISDOM FROM MY FATHER:

"Play it simple son. We have a right and a left pocket in our pants for a reason when we go to the casino. Put what you can afford to lose in one pocket, which means what you would have spent on a special night out not gambling and NO MORE than that. Then, put money in the other pocket for eating something nice. You will feel more enjoyment and excitement making it a special occasion with a friend or a loved one, rather than viewing this as a regular visit as if it were your job to hit the jackpot!

Gambling permeates our society in many different forms. If an individual is having a problem with gambling, there are different addiction treatment programs available along with educational and informational resources for teens and young adults about compulsive gambling. A great resource providing specific recovery programs across the U.S. is available at www.soberrecovery.com.

"You got to know when to hold 'em and know when to fold 'em!"

-Kenny Rogers

4. SPEEDING

Young drivers are one of the most vulnerable groups of drivers on the road. Teen drivers have the highest fatal crash risk of any age group. Being "behind the wheel" takes on a whole new meaning of responsibility that should be taken seriously. The movies have glamorized taking a spin and driving down the fast lane to escape the scene of the crime or save a person in distress and then reach their destination unscathed.

Reality speaks! Although drivers aged 17-25 represent just 16% of the current road users, they make up over a third of all speeding fatalities. Despite the fact that magazines, television, and cinema commercials have advertised youth road safety, hundreds of young drivers (17-25 years) are involved in speeding crashes that have terminated in death and the number continues to rise each year. In the United States, an average of 10 teenagers are killed in teen-driven vehicles every day (Watsford, 2008).

According to the National Transportation Safety Board statistics:

- Motor vehicle crashes remain the leading cause of death for 15-to-20 year olds.

- The risk of a crash involving a teenage driver increases with each additional teen passenger in a vehicle.

- Young drivers do only 20% of their driving at night, but over half the crash fatalities of adolescent drivers occur during nighttime hours.

*Source: NHTSA (2008).

Young drivers must be aware of their actions and possible consequences that can result from reckless driving. We depend on drivers to make responsible, law-abiding decisions on the road and for law enforcement to uphold these standards for the safety of all drivers. A car can be utilized unknowingly as a very destructive piece of equipment that can tear apart families in a blink of an eye. Destiny can be altered by split second decisions that are made on the road. How can the message to "take it easy on the road" be addressed and monitored effectively? First off, adults must understand why speeding is such a temptation among today's youth.

Why do so many teens feel the need for speed?

> ➤ TEEN BRAINS ARE NOT FULLY DEVELOPED.

Medical experts have discovered that the area of the brain that weighs risks in situations and controls impulsive behavior is not fully developed until age 25. The Insurance Institute for Highway Safety (IIHS) reports that 16-year-olds are at the highest risk among youth drivers. More than two-thirds of fatal single-vehicle teen crashes involved nighttime driving or at least one passenger aged 16 to 19. Nearly three-fourths of the drivers in those crashes were male. And 16-year-old drivers were the riskiest of all. Their rate of involvement in fatal crashes was nearly five times that of drivers aged 20 and older, according to the Insurance Institute for Highway Safety. Some state legislators are questioning whether 16-years-old is too young to receive a driver's license, considering that New Jersey has not allowed 16-year-olds to get a license to drive and they have the lowest teen fatality rate in all of the United States. In most European countries, a person must be 17 or 18-years-old in order to get a driver's license for a car (IIHS, 2008).

Risk factors associated with speed-related crashes:

- INEXPERIENCE BEHIND THE WHEEL

  It takes time and experience to acquire the necessary skills and judgment to become a proficient driver. A young driver's ability to handle a variety of situations rests in the matter of this much needed experience. Couple this fact with having another passenger in a car and talking on the phone and the hazardousness of the situation greatly increases. Forty percent of 16-year-old drivers involved in deadly single-vehicle crashes have one or more teen passengers. This age group pushes the limits the most and takes many risks. Decision-making skills are still maturing. Each year driving makes a big difference on the road to gain more experience and cognitive maturation (Wagner, 2005).

- TALKING/TEXTING ON THE PHONE WHILE DRIVING

Even though cell phone use while driving has been banned in many states in the U.S., teens are still on the phone talking/ texting and often times with another passenger, not paying attention to the road. According to a University of North Carolina at Chapel Hill study, drivers talking/texting on cell phones are twice as likely as other drivers not talking/texting on the phone involved in crashes to have rear-end collisions. A common violation for these drivers involved in the crash was failure to reduce speed. Data collected on the effect of hands-free devices versus hand-held devices fails to show a significant difference in risk of an injury crash. Revolutionary technology has developed an ignition key to prevent young people from text messaging and talking on the phone while driving. Time will indicate the tool's effectiveness for preventing phone-related accidents (University of Utah, 2009).

- DRIVING AT NIGHTTIME

Between 9 P.M. and 6 A.M. is when teen drivers are at a three times greater risk for getting into a fatal crash compared to drivers 20-years-old and over. Driving into unknown and more dangerous regions late at night is common for many teens. The IIHS states that 16-years-olds die at twice the rate at night as they do during the daytime and that crashes and fatalities are peaked on the weekends. Difficulty seeing the roads, staying alert, and reacting to unforeseen obstacles are major factors that contribute to fatal crashes during the nighttime. Drivers that drive drowsy especially risk with fate and often times overestimate their capabilities on the road. The National Highway Traffic Safety Administration (NHTSA) has found that males are 5 times more likely than females to be involved in drowsy driving crashes and individuals under 30-years-old account for one-quarter of all licensed drivers. Two-thirds of these crashes are reported from drivers under 30-years-old (Wagner, 2005).

- DRIVING IN UNSUITABLE VEHICLES

Safety has little to do with what teens want to drive. It is usually the coolest looking automobile that has a young driver's attention. Many parents have their teenager driving a compact car — which is the most unsafe vehicle in collisions with very large vehicles, such as a small pickup truck or a sports-utility vehicle (SUV) which tends to be top-heavy and less-than-desirable for safety records (Wagner, 2005).

- DRIVING WITH PASSENGERS

Driving with passengers in a vehicle poses a serious distraction to a young driver. Fatal crashes among teens are more likely to occur when other teenagers are in a car. The risk increases with every additional passenger. According to the National Commission Against Drunk Driving, 65% of teen passenger deaths happen in vehicles driven by another teenager (Wagner, 2005).

- MASS MEDIA

Evidence has clearly demonstrated the impact that mass media has on today's youth in so many areas. The need for speed is a common theme for many video games on the market along with various action-packed movies that spark interest in today's generation of thrill-seeking street racers. According to the NHTSA, street racing was listed as a factor in fatal crashes and was nearly double the amount in 2001 (ironically the year that *The Fast and the Furious* was released) as compared to 2000 statistics (Wagner, 2005).

- FAILURE TO WEAR A SEAT BELT

  According to the NHTSA, 57% of 16 to 20-year-old passenger vehicle occupants not wearing safety belts are killed in automobile crashes. Teen drivers have the lowest estimated buckle-up rate out of all age groups where approximately one in three fail to wear a seat belt while driving (NHTSA, 2008).

- RISKY BEHAVIORS

  Alcohol use and illegal-drug use are two major factors that contribute to teen death. According to the Substance Abuse and Mental Health Services Administration, 17% of all people ages 16-20 reported driving under the influence of alcohol and according to a recent *Monitoring the Future* survey conducted, 1 in 6 high school seniors reported driving under the influence of marijuana. The statistics about drunk/drugged and driving are alarming and is a major issue among today's youth (NIDA, 2008).

Advice for adults to help children curb the need for speed and keep it slow:

- Educate a child on the above risks mentioned. When a child clearly understands the consequences that could take place in each situation, the percentage substantially drops for risk of a speed-related crash.

- Be a role model driver for a child. Understand that a child is aware of how you drive and all of your habits. Set positive examples by abiding by the laws of the road. These consistent actions will help develop and ingrain safe driving skills and habits. Driver education classes may not be adequate enough to develop the necessary habits for the road. Taking a teenager out to drive will help her/him pay attention to detail and practice the proper habits of driving. Additionally, it can be an opportunity to reinforce the potential consequences of risky driving.

- Monitor a child's dealings with her/his friends and the people that she/he rides with in vehicles. Being aware of these details will increase the likelihood that a child will make good decisions with whomever she/he chooses to ride.

- Set a child up for success by providing her/him with a car that is safe. Emphasize that driving is a privilege and that a car is a vehicle used for transportation and that other drivers on the road depend on her/him to make responsible decisions. Point out that what a child is receiving from you is something that needs to be attended to with great care.

- Provide leadership roles at school for students to communicate the messages of safe driving with other students. When students have a voice and can actively participate in meaningful discussions, much can be accomplished and influenced on peers.

- Teach children the value of life. Stressing the importance of behaving with good morals and values and taking into consideration safety for yourself and others are fundamental to character building.

- Track a child with a global positioning system (GPS) chip that is inserted into a car and/or a child's cell phone that detects where she/he is and how fast she/he is driving. It is a parent's responsibility to keep an eye on a child and at a "close range" if there is suspicion of any wrongdoing. Many times the act of repetitive speeding is a sign of other risky lifestyle behaviors.

Speeding is preventable! If something out of the ordinary were to happen while driving fast, one's reaction time would not be quick enough to make the best choice to avoid an accident — even though one may think so. Within seconds, a driver's life, another person's life, and their families will forever be scarred because of a careless decision made. Is this fair to anyone, especially the innocent party on the receiving end of the blow?

We hear about these tragic events occurring all too frequently and compounded with mind-altering drugs such as alcohol or marijuana while speeding behind a wheel and not even recalling events that took place. The word "devastating" does not even begin to accurately address the severity of the case. It is the responsibility of today's parents, educators, and mentors to ensure that young people follow the driving laws carefully and respect the rights of others on the road — valuing life. Teaching a child about the difference between "good driving" and "safe driving" can save many lives.

5. SEX

Studies show that approximately half of all high school students (9th-12th grade) had sexual intercourse and 65% will by the time they graduate (Rector et al., 2003). Our society glamorizes this kind of behavior as is evidenced by various soap operas, sitcoms, reality TV shows, movies, and music. Keep in mind that the media is a mogul that wants young people's attention so that they are able to grab onto their parents' money. The media's concern is least about the welfare and future of a child.

As a child enters secondary school (6th, 7th, 8th grade), hormones are in full force and choices involving relationships with the opposite sex become more serious. Sex education in school discusses the risks involved when engaging in sexual behaviors at a young age and potential consequences. Unlike any other activity, having sex can create life-altering situations ranging from contracting a sexually transmitted disease (STD) to being forced to grow up faster than expected and becoming a parent to a child. Going out freely, partying, having fun, and achieving dreams become a distant thought and a far-reaching possibility for a young parent. Feeding a child and affording for her/his needs on a daily basis become reality.

Sexual activity among teens is connected to substantial problems with emotional health. Studies suggest that there is a relationship between teen sexual activity and depression and suicide — but which is the cause and which is the effect is unclear. Substantial data does not demonstrate, for certain, that early sexual activity leads to either or both of the two, but the significantly lower levels of happiness and higher levels of depression among sexually active teens lead to an increase in emotional stress and reduction in happiness and overall well-being. However, various social forces may play a role such as a child's socioeconomic background, which may contribute to emotional stress and instability leading to more sexually active behaviors. Other factors such as race, gender, family income, and age have been compared and they did not have a significant effect on this link between teen sexual activity and depression/suicide (Rector et al., 2003).

Adolescent sexual activity is also associated with decreased academic performance, lowered self-esteem, and an increase in relationship violence, drug, and alcohol abuse. Although sexual activity among teenagers has decreased in recent years, it is still a widespread problem. According to the Center for Disease Control and Prevention (CDC), a reported 46.8% of high school students across the U.S. engaged in sexual intercourse and 30% of these students reported having four or more partners thus far. Over one-third (34.3%) of 9th graders reported having sexual experience (Harr, 2006).

Why are so many teenagers choosing to be sexually active?

Teenagers respond to their family life and school life in a variety of ways. For many teens, having sex is a means to medicate their beings. It is a perceived solution for acquiring happiness in their lives for where they feel it is lacking. The link between increased sexual activity and a low-income background, little or no parental supervision at home, difficulty in school with grades, and relationships with peers trigger premature sexual activity.

Consider the following example that I could safely say expresses how an overwhelmingly high number of teens feel prior to engaging in sexual activity.

"Jane" is 16-years-old and "Mike" is 17-years-old. They have been dating for a few months and think that they love each other. They decide that they want to take their relationship to the next level. They both see the next step as having sex. They have concerns about this, but are both afraid to express them. They don't know much about sex and its consequences. They remember being taught something in junior high about the risks of STDs and unwanted pregnancies, but were not really paying close attention to it all. They did hear from various sources on television, in the movies, and from friends about how much fun and how good it feels having sex. They are just not sure if they should avoid reality ignoring the consequences, hoping they will go away because it couldn't possibly happen to them, or take responsibility and get some information about safe sex.

Where can "Jane" and "Mike" go to get information? Experts highlight the importance of the parent-child relationship and advise for parents to openly discuss the topic of sex with their child. If parents had a good communication relationship with their child, then sexual activity and pregnancy levels would be lower (Rector et al., 2004). Nevertheless, this is not always the reality.

Teenagers need to receive accurate information from significant others. This is easier said than done since many parents do not feel comfortable addressing this issue of sex. In cases of poor parent-child relationships, government agencies and organizations are making it possible for teens to find out information on contraceptives without their parents' permission. Comprehensive sex education classes in school discuss and often times promote the use of contraceptives, rather than emphasize a strong abstinence message in which parents support.

> **MYTH:**   Messages of abstinence for young people are unrealistic and an ineffective means of education.
>
> *FACT*:   Abstinence education programs are highly effective in reducing teen sexual activity.

According to recently released data from the National Longitudinal Study of Adolescent Health, abstinence organizations such as "True Love Waits" have encouraged young people for over a decade to make a verbal or written pledge that they will abstain from sex until marriage. This commitment may sound ineffective and non-educational, but statistics show that virgin females who take this pledge are 40% less likely to have a child before marriage, as compared to similar young women who do not take the pledge. This holds true when all social forces are held constant (socioeconomic background, race, religion, etc.) (Rector et al., 2004).

Depression and Sexual Activity

	Never/Rarely Depressed	Depressed Sometimes	Depressed A Lot	Depressed Most/ All of the Time
BOYS 14-17				
Sexually Active	63.3%	28.4%	5.0%	3.3%
Not Sexually Active	76.2%	20.3%	2.6%	0.8%
GIRLS 14-17				
Sexually Active	36.8%	37.9%	15.5%	9.8%
Not Sexually Active	60.2%	32.1%	4.9%	2.8%

Source: National Longitudinal Survey of Adolescent Health, Wave II (1996).

The Majority of Sexually Active Teens Wish They Had Waited Longer Before Beginning Sexual Activity

Wished They Had Waited Longer Before Starting Sexual Activity	All Sexually Active Teens	Sexually Active Boys	Sexually Active Girls
YES	63%	55%	72%
NO	32%	39%	25%

Source: National Longitudinal Survey of Adolescent Health, Wave II (1996).
Note: Survey covers sexually active teens aged 12 to 17.

Add alcohol and drug use to the mix and the numbers become quite disturbing.

Drinking and Risky Sexual Behavior

	TEENS 15 to 17	YOUNG ADULTS 18 to 24
Alcohol or drugs have influenced their decision to do something sexual	29%	37%
They have done more sexually than planned because they had been drinking or using drugs	24%	31%
They have worried about STDs or pregnancy because of something they did sexually while drinking or using drugs	26%	28%
They have used alcohol or drugs to help them feel more comfortable with a sexual partner	13%	16%
They have had unprotected sex because they were drinking or using drugs	12%	25%

Source: The Henry J. Kaiser Family Foundation and The National Center on Addiction and Substance Abuse at Columbia University. "Substance Abuse and Risky Behavior: Attitudes and Practices Among Adolescents and Young Adults." Survey Snapshot. (6 February 2002).

In a study conducted by the Kaiser Family Foundation, 23% (5.6 million) of sexually active teens and young adults ages 15-24 in the United States report having had unprotected sex because they were drinking or using drugs at the time. Twenty-four percent of teens (ages 15-17) say that their alcohol and drug use led them to be more sexual than they had intended (Kaiser, 2002). It was estimated that of the nearly 15 million new cases of sexually transmitted diseases each year, 25% (3.8 million cases) occur among youth ages 15-19. Teens who use alcohol are seven times more likely to be sexually active, putting them at a greater risk for STDs (CASA, 1999).

Proposed strategies for reducing teen sexual activity:

AT HOME...

- Build a strong, close relationship with a child from an early age. Listen to a child and encourage open discussions about any and all topics of life.

- Be clear about your own values about having sexual relationships at a young age. Think back to when you were your child's age. Helpful questions to ask yourself include: "Were you sexually active early on?" "How early on?" "What do you think about encouraging your child to abstain versus use contraceptives?"

- Discuss the theme of relationships and intimacy early on in a child's life. Having regular conversations with a child helps guide and inform her/him about these topics in which they may have a lot of questions.

- Work in accordance with the school program and ask a health education teacher for any literature that can help provide tips on how to discuss this topic most effectively with your child.

- Discourage early, frequent, and steady dating. Voice your opinion clearly and hold to a standard that you have deemed age-appropriate to begin dating. Group activities among young people are fine and fun, but dating before 16 can lead to problems — especially if the other person in the relationship is older. Many families' dating age begins at 18-years-old or following the graduation of high school. Discuss pregnancy prevention by addressing various contraceptives available. As awkward as the situation may seem at the moment, the repercussions for not firmly addressing these issues will be quite severe, not just for a child, but also for you and other family members.

- If your child is in her/his college years, re-emphasize your values. If a child is entering into a steady relationship, communicate for her/him to be proactive. Set the limits in the relationship and discuss potential consequences of people who have not taken preventive action.

AT SCHOOLS...

- All middle/junior high schools should have a comprehensive sex education program that clearly promotes a strong abstinence message with an unbiased and fact-based discussion on safe sex, various modes of contraception, and potential consequences of pre-marital sex.

- Students should be given various case studies to solve and analyze the situations discussing the risks involved and the unfortunate outcomes of the situations.

- Programs should include child-parent interactions so a child and/or a parent do not feel awkward approaching the topic alone. Making it mandatory for a child to get parental feedback about various cases and/or obtaining signatures showing that a parent has discussed the case with a child would help open the communication lines between a parent and a child.

- Programs should promote discussion from students and a teacher should answer any questions to the best of her/his ability.

- Programs should bring in a guest speaker who is willing to discuss real-life mistakes made, regrets, and consequences from engaging in sexual activity before marriage.

Caring and intimacy promote commitment. Sexual desire and activity should be a natural byproduct of a strong, already developed intimacy. It is important that a child distinguish between having sex and being intimate with another person. The latter emotion focuses on sharing a mutual emotional interest in each other and some sort of history together, demonstrating a long-term commitment to one another, supporting one another reciprocally during good and bad times, expressing feelings openly and honestly, viewing a partner as most trustworthy, a confidante and best friend, and envisioning a continued relationship with hopes and dreams for the future.

6. DIVORCE

Divorce is a painful process and unfortunately, is still quite prevalent. Couples divorce due to a wide array of reasons that include macro-level explanations involving cultural values, shift in gender roles, technology boom, and social institutions. Demographic variables such as one's race, ethnicity, socioeconomic status, education, age at marriage, premarital childbearing, and parental divorce often times contribute to the decision of one's divorce (Benokraitis, 2008).

Are divorces beneficial or harmful for children?

Divorces can bring out the worst in people and when children are involved, they hear sometimes cruel, hurtful things being said about their own parent. These messages are very uncomfortable to hear and can become self-destructive for a parent and unfair and hurtful for a child being exposed to such verbal hostility.

Adults are affected by divorce emotionally, psychologically, physically, socially, and financially at many different levels. It is important that a divorced individual recognize and begin to overcome whatever loss she/he is experiencing the greatest. Involved children are often caught in the middle of hostility and pain before and after the divorce from one or both parents. Many studies have shown that children from divorced families exhibit a multitude of difficulties including lower academic achievement, behavioral problems, a lower self-concept, and some long-term health problems (Thornberry et al., 1999; Furstenberg and Kiernan, 2001).

If you or anyone you know is going through a divorce, objectively analyze the following actions below. If you agree that any or many of these statements apply, then eliminating them as quickly as possible will make the difference for how a child adjusts to divorce.

➤ Treating a child as a peer discussing a wide array of personal issues using her/him as a shoulder to cry on.

➤ Expressing bitter, negative emotions to a child about the other parent consciously or unconsciously.

➢ Putting all of the blame on the other parent for the divorce.

➢ Seeing a child less and less as the non-custodial parent.

➢ Asking a child for information about the other parent.

➢ Using child support as a means to control the other parent into allowing visitation rights.

➢ Not paying for child support because you feel shut out of the family, economically hard pressed, desire revenge, or are unwilling to fulfill your parental duties.

➢ Becoming more involved with new relationships, whether intimately or finding new friends, and less interested in a child's day-to-day activities.

➢ Being chronically depressed in front of a child and unable to fulfill family responsibilities that you used to such as going to work on time, cleaning the house, making regular meals, holding high expectations for a child, etc.

➢ Buying a child whatever she/he wants and/or giving in to unreasonable demands because you feel guilty about the divorce.

How can divorced parents best help their child through this difficult time?

Parents should openly communicate the situation with their child. The decision to get a divorce should not be a surprise received without warning to a child. After discussing memories of a divorce with older children and adult children, they recall feelings of shock and anger, feeling lied to, when they thought everything was happy. Research indicates that such children may avoid intimate relationships because they expect a partner to be unpredictable or undependable (Benokraitis, 2008).

Children need to hear that their parents will always love them and that the parent-child relationship continues despite the marriage coming to an end. The message should be clear that the decision to get a divorce was strictly due to happenings between the parents and not the child. Over 80% of all custodies for raising a child are sole —meaning that one parent has sole responsibility for raising the child, which 85% of the time is the mother, and the other parent has specified visitation rights (Benokraitis, 2008).

It is important that a child regularly sees his non-custodial parent. Unfortunately, a mere 18% of biological non-custodial fathers are involved in their child's life, in school affairs, aware of their peer group, and present to help them make important life decisions (Benokraitis, 2008; Stewart, 1999; Hetherington and Kelly, 2002; Grall, 2003).

Much research indicates that a father who maintains close ties with his child can reestablish the child's trust in the father and other adults. If the father is abusive or has other major problems, then it is best for the child and mother to have minimal contact with him (Aseltine and Kessler, 1993; King, 1994).

Violence can take on many forms where children experience physical and mental abuse in the form of neglect, sexual, and verbal abuse. Divorce brings many changes for a child and adults. It is important through this trying time that parents demonstrate a healthy attitude and respect for one another. Creating a peaceful, stable environment is very important for a child's well being (Gilligan, 2001).

A child put in the middle of parental quarrels often develops feelings of bitterness and experiences difficulties later in life with relationships. Parents have the power to create a comfortable atmosphere that teaches a child much about life. Whether a child chooses love over hate is largely up to parents and how these messages are transmitted via parent-to-parent or parent-to-child.

How do children gain a sense of security through this time of change?

Many young children do not have the level of maturity necessary to fully comprehend the circumstances of a divorce. A child's perception and understanding of a divorce will change over time.

Tips for parents/guardians to best help a child cope with a divorce:

- The message must be stated clearly that the decision to get a divorce was made strictly because of differences between the two parents and has nothing to do with their child.

- Parents should provide a clear, concise explanation to their child to help her/him best understand the reason behind the divorce.

- Parents should be good listeners and realize that the reaction to the divorce can be a wide variety of emotions and to be supportive and listen patiently answering any questions or clarifying any specific concerns.

- Reinforce the fact that you are proud of your child and that you love her/him very much. Children need to feel loved.

- Children involved must be made aware that even though their parents may disagree on certain things, they are and always will be loved by both parents, despite the divorce.

- Parents should never expect their children to be their emotional saddle. Another parent or adult member of the family should never speak badly about a parent of a child. This indirectly forces a child to choose a side and have stronger feelings for one parent over the other. Rather, support relationships with the other parent unless there is a serious threat to the physical or emotional well-being from that parent.

- Be nurturing, caring, and consistent in your ways. It is important to provide a stable environment with clear rules and expectations; this provides structure to a child's life. Reassure the child that she/he is safe and secure.

- Respectfully discuss a parenting plan for the child. Be flexible and willing to compromise with the other parent. Put aside differences and look out for the interests of your child.

Therefore, being understanding and proactive in constructing a parenting plan will work towards everyone's advantage in the long run.

- Assure that a child will still see her/his grandparents on both sides of the family.

- If you are a single parent, you may be overwhelmed by the responsibility of handling it all. Recruit a trusting, caring support system around you that can help.

- You must take care of yourself FIRST! You (and your child) must realize that you are only one person taking care of the family. Provide your child tasks/chores to be completed. This teaches a child responsibility and takes some of the pressures off your day-to-day tasks.

Divorce is often thought of as taboo in our society and that there cannot be any positive outcomes. Some experts in the field advise parents to remain in unhappy marriages for the sake of the children — for the fear that the children will become dysfunctional as adults. In contrast, most divorced couples and their children adjust and function well over time (Montenegro, 2004).

The major positive outcome of divorce is the release from an unhappy, miserable situation. The built up frustrations and stresses accumulated over a prolonged time (most likely) are released and improve the psyche of both parents and their children. If parents handled divorces in more rational and thoughtful ways, many children would be spared additional emotional despair. Divorce can provide parents and children with new opportunities for personal growth and to live a more pleasant family life. More than anything, the determining factor in how well a child adjusts to divorce is how well a parent continues to parent after the divorce.

7. PRESCRIPTION DRUGS

Non-medical use and abuse of prescription drugs has become one of the fastest growing addictions among today's youth. Hospitals are receiving more cases in the emergency room of young people overdosing on combinations of prescription medicines. The Partnership for a Drug-Free America (PDFA) has coined the term describing this generation of substance abuse among teens and young adults as "Generation Rx." An estimated one in every five teenagers in the United States has abused legal painkillers. Prescription painkillers such as OxyContin, Vicodin, Percocet, and Codeine have become popular prescription drugs of choice providing a numb, euphoric effect (Prescription Medicine Abuse, 2008).

A reported one in five teens abuse prescription stimulants and tranquilizers. Stimulants such as Ritalin, Adderall, and Dexedrine are being used more frequently to increase energy levels and achieve a euphoric state, especially by older teens and college students. A reported one in ten teens/young adults has abused cough medicine to achieve a hallucinogenic effect. In addition, household cleaners such as glue, paint thinner, nail polish remover, and other solvents are being abused for their intoxicating effects (Prescription Medicine Abuse, 2008).

How do kids know what to do with prescription drugs? Teens have admitted that they get ideas from the Internet, sharing their experiences with other peers, and simply experimenting and seeing what happens. They feel invincible and do not truly think about the consequences that could happen. Adolescents have what has been termed "Pharm" parties. They have become a popular means where kids bring all of their prescription drugs that they have and experiment with different types. Often times, this type of abuse goes unnoticed among parents (Leinwand, 2006).

The abuse of legally prescribed drugs by today's youth is seen as a way to get around the restrictions and laws. The availability and access to get these products are much easier considering that many families have left over pills in their medicine cabinets from a surgery or illness. The casual theft from home and transactions on and off school property make it very easy for these drugs to get around. Many Internet pharmacies are distributing these drugs without much of a medical consultation. Some kids go as far as faking to be sick in order to acquire some medication.

Here are statements from teens and young adults concerning prescription drug use:

"It's just easier to pop a pill at school without people noticing."

"It's more socially acceptable."

"They are easy to get from home."

"I used it for a prescription and then it became addicting."

"These are medicines. It's much safer than doing bad drugs."

"They don't smell on your breath or body so they are easy to hide."

"There are a lot of doctors' kids who can get copies of the prescription form."

How do kids use these drugs?

- Swallow the pills.

- Crush the pills and snort them.

- Crush the pills and take them with a drink.

- Smoke the powder.

Potential results from sustained periods of abuse include (Krimsky and Peck, 2005):

➢ Respiratory failure,
➢ Permanent brain damage,
➢ Depression,
➢ Heart attacks,

➢ Seizures,
➢ Frequent mood shifts,
➢ Hostility,
➢ Paranoia,
➢ Anxiety,
➢ Nausea,
➢ Diarrhea,
➢ Muscle and bone pain,
➢ Restlessness,
➢ Liver damage,
➢ Kidney damage,
➢ Other organ injuries.

According to the PDFA, there are three categories of prescription drugs being misused: pain medications, amphetamines, and sedatives (sedative-hypnotics and tranquilizers) (Krimsky and Peck, 2005).

A partial listing follows:

Pain medications:

Vicodin, OxyContin, Percocet, Percodan, Darvon, Darvocet, Dilaudid, Tylox, Lortab, Lorcet, Codeine.

Amphetamines:

Ritalin, Concerta, Adderall, Focalin, Dexedrine, Meridia.

Sedatives:

Valium, Xanax, Ativan, Klonopin, Restoril, Ambien, Lunesta, Mebaral, Nembutal, Librium.

*Over-the-counter products:

Household cleaners, cough syrup, decongestants (pseudoephedrine — which is used as a key ingredient needed for the production of the illicit drug methamphetamine).

*An added category of products abused by teens and young adults.

Prescription drugs are next in line behind marijuana as most frequently used by young individuals. They are inexpensive compared to illicit drugs, widely available, and easily accessible. When abused, these drugs can alter brain activity and give an individual a false sense of a "high" — resulting in irreversible damage over the long term. Abusers may experience a heightened state of arousal, euphoria, energy, but this dangerous behavior can lead to serious long-term problems both mentally and physically (Prescription For Danger, 2008).

As I stated, many middle/junior high and high school students have the ability to easily access these drugs from their own homes and then enter school and distribute them during lunch, in the bathrooms, in locker rooms, after school on or off school grounds, at friends' homes, on the streets, at parties, or through Internet sales. Young people commonly abuse tranquilizers, stimulants, pain relievers, and even glue for many reasons that include being popular, foolishly curious, and/or having family troubles. They hear about cases of students dying from an overdose of pills, yet they continue to abuse these drugs.

Turning this troubling trend around — Tips to help prevent children from abusing prescription drugs:

- Discuss the use for prescription medicine and educate a child on the dangers that these can have, if taken without reason. Prescription medicine is powerful and can benefit a sick person, but it can have a drastically negative effect on a healthy person. Emphasize that prescription drug abuse can be just as addictive and lethal as illicit drug abuse. For example, painkillers are made from opioids, the same substance found in heroin.

- Be active in a child's life and monitor the group of friends that she/he associates with. Discard leftover medications and urge friends' parents to either hide or dispose their medications, also.

- Keep all prescription medicine hidden. Rather than keeping it in a typical medicine cabinet, put it in a less conspicuous area.

If you suspect that a child has taken some, take an inventory count and monitor pill quantities and medicine levels.

- Educate children on the misconception that prescription medicine use is safer than illegal, street drugs because doctors approve prescription drugs. A school resource officer can speak to individuals, groups of children, classrooms, and/or the entire school about making good choices and addressing the dangers and consequences involved in this type of drug use.

- Government programs should be instituted across the nation educating parents, schools, and law enforcement about speaking to youth about the dangers of drug abuse, including prescription drugs.

- Monitor a child's activities on the computer, the time spent on the computer, and limit the places available to surf.

- Schools should have inclusive classes that focus on life skills, social skills, and good decision-making.

- Monitor a child's behaviors. Look for some observable warning signs of abuse.

Signs include:

- ➢ Drop in grades.
- ➢ Chronic absence from school.
- ➢ Being frequently sick.
- ➢ Change in group of friends.
- ➢ Change in mood, eating patterns and overall attitude.
- ➢ Failure to cooperate and frequently breaks rules set forth.
- ➢ Disappearance of medication, money and/or credit cards.
- ➢ Appearance of strange paraphernalia: pipes, rolling papers, small medicine droppers, eye drops, bongs, butane lighters.

Like all illicit drug abuse, using prescription drugs for the wrong reasons can result in many serious consequences for an individual.

There are several options available for successfully treating an addiction to prescription drugs. The Substance Abuse Treatment Facility Locator spans more than 12,000 treatment centers. To find a treatment center in the U.S., visit http://findtreatment.samhsa.gov/facilitylocatordoc. htm.

8.   SUBSTANCE ABUSE

Most parents had or will have a discussion about the dangers involved in drug use.   Teachers educate children on the negative impacts that illicit drugs have in the world.   Commercials on television have expressed the problems associated with doing drugs.   Health shows and biography stories on television and in books discuss the gloomy road and ill effects that many people have traveled.   At schools, guest speakers talk about their sad, arduous journey battling drug addiction. Moreover, recovering family members impregnate the message into a young relative's head through examples and/or words of wisdom: DON'T DO DRUGS!

Children at one point or another at school probably signed a banner or a contract of some sort pledging a life-long commitment to be drug-free.   Young people are fully aware of the dangers and consequences involved — no question about it.   In spite of it all, a problem persists with drug abuse among today's youth.   How can this be?

There is a greater supply of drugs today than there has ever been in our world's history.   People are able to obtain them from closer to home, as opposed to the illegal smuggling that ran so rampant from various parts of Central and South America.   Marijuana is still ranked as the most popular drug of choice where approximately one in two 12th graders have admitted to trying it at least once and 29% reported current use.   The effects of this drug are frequently overlooked. Considered the "gateway drug," its active intoxicating chemical ingredient is THC (tetrahydrocannabinol), which alters the functions of various nerve cells in the brain to produce a high feeling (NIDA, 2005).

Some of the club or party drugs that have gained popularity include MDMA (Ecstasy), GHB, Rohypnol, ketamine, methamphetamine, and LSD.   Research has shown that use of these drugs are linked to an increase in reports of sexual assaults committed by "slipping someone's drink."   The dangers of these drugs are augmented when taken in combination with alcoholic beverages (Club drugs, 2000).

The effects that drugs have on children at school are what concern parents and educators.   Drugs alter moods, reduce a child's ability to focus at school, increase sickness and days absent from school, affect organization and ability to follow through on assignments, diminish motivation, and may create changes in brain development that put youth at risk for becoming addicted to other drugs (Marijuana, 2009). Adults are begging for answers to help prevent children from becoming hooked on drugs.

Why do so many young people fall victim to experimenting with something that has never been documented in any scientific research journal across the world as being helpful in building up one's health over a long time with its prolonged use? Granted there have been select cases of various drugs such as morphine being prescribed to ease pain for patients who have undergone surgery or marijuana as having some potential medicinal uses, but the adverse effects of marijuana on the respiratory system outweigh the benefits of smoked marijuana (for these patients) (NIDA, 2005).

Is it that young people believe that they are invincible and that anyone besides them is a mere mortal? To state to young people, point blank, that they are human beings and will age like the rest of the *Homo sapiens* that have come before us on this planet. They must be aware that the human body is not indestructible and early damage can have a later, more severe impact. Unfortunately, this message does not always sink in as something that is relevant to their lives.

How can we carve this message into the minds of youth? Caring adults must make it their mission to try and best understand the pressure-packed choices that children have to make day in and day out that affect how they are perceived among their peers and how they are treated. This understanding allows for an adult to better relate to a child and address the specific needs. The secret lies in frequent and open communication with a child to unlock a potentially successful future.

The Reality of Drug Abuse

Percentage of 8th-Graders Who Have Used Marijuana: Monitoring the Future Study, 2007

	1994	1995	1996	1997	1998	1999	2000
Lifetime	16.7%	19.9%	23.1%	22.6%	22.2%	22.0%	20.3%
Past Year	13.0	15.8	18.3	17.7	16.9	16.5	15.6
Past Month	7.8	9.1	11.3	10.2	9.7	9.7	9.1
Daily	0.7	0.8	1.5	1.1	1.1	1.4	1.3

	2001	2002	2003	2004	2005	2006	2007
Lifetime	20.4%	19.2%	17.5%	16.3%	16.5%	15.7	14.2
Past Year	15.4	14.6	12.8	11.8	12.2	11.7	10.3
Past Month	9.2	8.3	7.5	6.4	6.6	6.5	5.7
Daily	1.3	1.2	1.0	0.8	1.0	1.0	0.8

Percentage of 10th-Graders Who Have Used Marijuana: Monitoring the Future Study, 2007

	1994	1995	1996	1997	1998	1999	2000
Lifetime	30.4%	34.1%	39.8%	42.3%	39.6%	40.9%	40.3%
Past Year	25.2	28.7	33.6	34.8	31.1	32.1	32.2
Past Month	15.8	17.2	20.4	20.5	18.7	19.4	19.7
Daily	2.2	2.8	3.5	3.7	3.6	3.8	3.8

	2001	2002	2003	2004	2005	2006	2007
Lifetime	40.1%	38.7%	36.4%	35.1%	34.1%	31.8%	31.0%
Past Year	32.7	30.3	28.2	27.5	26.6	25.2	24.6
Past Month	19.8	17.8	17.0	15.9	15.2	14.2	14.2
Daily	4.5	3.9	3.6	3.2	3.1	2.8	2.8

**Percentage of 12th-Graders Who Have Used Marijuana
Monitoring the Future Study, 2007**

	1994	1995	1996	1997	1998	1999	2000
Lifetime	38.2%	41.7%	44.9%	49.6%	49.1%	49.7%	48.8%
Past Year	30.7	34.7	35.8	38.5	37.5	37.8	36.5
Past Month	19.0	21.2	21.9	23.7	22.8	23.1	21.6
Daily	3.6	4.6	4.9	5.8	5.6	6.0	6.0

	2001	2002	2003	2004	2005	2006	2007
Lifetime	49.0%	47.8%	46.1%	45.7%	44.8%	42.3%	41.8%
Past Year	37.0	36.2	34.9	34.3	33.6	31.5	31.7
Past Month	22.4	21.5	21.2	19.9	19.8	18.3	18.8
Daily	5.8	6.0	6.0	5.6	5.0	5.0	5.1

"Lifetime" refers to use at least once during a respondent's lifetime. "Past year" refers to use at least once during the year preceding an individual's response to the survey. "Past month" refers to use at least once during the 30 days preceding an individual's response to the survey.

*Source: *2007 Monitoring the Future survey, funded by the National Institute on Drug Abuse, National Institutes of Health, DHHS, and conducted annually by the University of Michigan's Institute for Social Research. The survey has tracked 12th graders' illicit drug use and related attitudes since 1975; in 1991, 8th and 10th graders were added to the study. The latest data are online at www.drugabuse.gov. For street terms searchable by drug name, street term, cost and quantities, drug trade, and drug use, visit: http://www.whitehousedrugpolicy.gov/streetterms/default.asp.*

TORMENTS that "can be prescribed" for drug abuse
(Volkow, 2007):

➤ Disturbed energy levels, which contribute to a lack of motivation to do much of anything.
➤ Disrupted concentration in class, homework completion, study time, and efficiency.
➤ Impaired memory for learning information.
➤ Altered respiration and heart rates.
➤ Changed physical composition of the cells and the hereditary material, which can alter one's life span.
➤ Potential drastic mood swings (highs followed by extreme lows (e.g. euphoric states followed by a strong wave of depression/ having suicidal notions).
➤ Insomnia.
➤ Impotence.
➤ Organ damage.
➤ High blood pressure.
➤ Convulsions.
➤ DEATH!

The typical discussion of the potential dangers involved in doing drugs has been ingrained in a child's head from early elementary school and continues throughout high school.

Questions that parents and educators can ask children utilizing a more critical thinking approach when faced to make the right decision:

❖ Will you allow others' perceptions of you and words to affect your decision-making? Why?

❖ Why should you ever turn to drugs to satisfy others' view of you and ruin the rest of your life? Explain.

❖ Do you dream of growing up to be a drug addict? Why do people start when they have seen the effects of drug use at school, on television, in movies, and among celebrities?

❖ Why do some individuals your age not think about the harmful effects that drugs will have on them when they get older? Have you ever seen first-hand the effects that drugs have on a person? Is that how you envision your future?

Who has control over your life? You or drugs? What about drug users?

Why do kids use drugs?

- Feel bad about themselves.
- Desire to feel accepted.
- Afraid to say no.
- Wish to feel good.
- Unestablished standards and ethics ingrained in a child.
- Curiosity.
- Boredom.
- Escape from painful situations at home, in school, and in the community.
- Rebellion against authority.
- Lack of self-discipline and control in one's life.
- Having anything desired because of overindulgence.

*Source: Talking With Kids About Drugs (2009).

What if you suspect a child is doing drugs?

Here are suggested statements to express to a child:

➤ *"I am worried that something different is going on in your life. You can always talk with me. I am here to listen to you."*

> ➢ *"Drugs are for weak people who do not have their own opinions and follow what other people say who don't wish good for your life."*

> ➢ *"I don't want to see you ruin your life because of a poor decision."*

> ➢ *"Doing drugs is a serious problem and let us solve it together."*

Note: If a child is abusing drugs, be prepared to have this discussion many times. If drug abuse continues to persist and it seems out of control, do not hesitate to admit the child into a hospital or rehabilitation program, immediately.   A useful website for searching for the best facility in your area is www.addictionsearch.com.

- *Strategies to help build strong character in a young child to help her/him handle life's challenges:*

- Provide clear guidelines for a child to follow. Teaching a child to follow rules and stay consistent to those expectations helps build a child's self-discipline.

- Be a role model to children and demonstrate the kind of behavior that you expect from them. Teaching a young child to tell the truth, play fairly, clean up, share toys, and say thank you are valuable habits that should be taught early on in life.

- Let a young child take on leadership roles in playing games and choosing what clothes she/he would like to wear to school (dress code appropriate). This reinforces a child's ability to be a leader and make good decisions.

- Point out harmful and poisonous substances that are commonly found in the house such as bleach, dishwasher detergent, fabric softeners, furniture polish, etc. and read the labels out loud.

- Have healthy foods in the house and discuss why healthy foods are important for their physical and mental health.

Allow a child to choose which foods they would like to see in a "healthy list" that you create at home with them.

- Don't make excuses for a child's actions. Address any undesirable behaviors immediately and replace it with something desirable. Especially as a child gets older, an adult is not helping a child by making excuses for undesirable actions, but rather enabling the behavior to persist. Children who are enabled get a rude awakening to the real world and often times fail to comply with rules or understand why they apply to them.

- If a child makes a mistake, discuss how it can be corrected. This shows a child that it is possible to make up for a wrongdoing and furthermore that she/he should correct a mistake that was made. Teaching a child to be accountable for her/his actions makes for better decision-making.

We are most influenced by what we visualize and hear in society. Showing a child the harsh realities of substance abuse and how an addicted individual suffers, along with family members, friends, and innocent others being affected, can have a great impact. Bringing guest speakers into a school discussing their history and the problems they faced as a result of their addiction can grasp the attention of children. If you feel that a child may be experimenting with drug use, it may be a good idea to sit down and have her/him also view a film based on a true story that displays a harsh reality of the road to drug addiction and beyond (e.g. *Rebound: The Legend of Earl "The Goat" Manigault* and *Basketball Diaries*).

The best time to discuss the harmful implications of drug use is as early as possible. Children develop their beliefs, attitudes, and values early on in life. Values are formed at a young age and have an impact on decisions made, as they get older. Parents have the most important role in impacting a young child's life and teaching her/him decision-making strategies and problem-solving skills vital to coping in society as a young person and an adult.

9. ALCOHOL

She was homecoming queen, class president, cheerleading captain, and honor student in high school. After attending the college's largest social event and a number of parties consuming somewhere between 30 and 40 beers in an 11-hour time frame, her friends left her alone to sleep it off in a fraternity house. The next day she was found dead while a fraternity member was giving his mother a tour (Dakss, 2004). This story is one of thousands of real-life stories of adolescents dying after a binge-drinking episode.

Half of all college students partake in these binge-drinking activities, consuming five or more drinks consecutively for males and four or more drinks in a row for females at least once or twice a week — which contribute to around 1700 deaths of young adults aged 18-24 per year in the United States. Alcohol is a factor in approximately 600,000 accidents and 100,000 cases of sexual assault or rape each year (College Binge Drinking, 2006).

Alcohol has been the cause of many premature deaths among youth. The leading cause of death among youth aged 15-20 is motor vehicle crashes and half of all teen automobile-related accidents involve the use of alcohol. Alcohol abuse is linked to as many as two-thirds of all sexual assaults and date rapes of teens and college students. This toxin contributes to youth suicides, homicides, and fatal accidents (e.g. falling off of balconies at parties). Add to the mix that alcohol is a poison and nutritionally devoid of vitamins and minerals that are required daily (RUDC, 2005).

Approximately ten million people who are under the legal drinking age of 21 consume alcohol in the U.S. It is the most popular drug used by high school seniors and college students (RUDC, 2005). According to Monitoring the Future (2005), nearly 80% of twelfth grade students reported having experimented with alcohol at least once as compared to 71% of tenth grade students and 52% of eighth grade students. In fact, 62% of twelfth graders, 49% of tenth graders, and 25% of eighth graders reported having been drunk at least once.

Half of all college students on campus engage in high-risk drinking (RUDC, 2005). This is often viewed as a rite of passage that one is "grown up" and "independent of parents."

Problems that can occur from abusing alcohol (Saisan et al., 2009):

- Doing irreversible physical damage to the body.
- Destroying relationships between partners and friends.
- Impairing academic performance.
- Reducing concentration and focus on tasks.
- Decreasing study time.
- Increasing truancy (missing classes at school).
- Ruining physique.
- Engaging in risky, disease-contracting sexual behaviors.
- Disturbing sleep patterns.
- Destroying brain cells.
- Having long-term health problems (ex. liver cirrhosis).
- Disappointing loved ones.
- Creating family stress.
- Putting a limit on one's future.

Statistics tell the bleak story resulting from binge drinking.

*Alcohol abuse contributes to:

- ➤ 28% of college dropouts.
- ➤ 66% of student suicides.
- ➤ 40% academic problems.
- ➤ 60% of STDs (including HIV).

- "Approximately 87% of college students who do not participate in binge drinking have experienced problems caused by their peers abusing alcohol, including physical assault, sexual harassment and abuse, disrupted sleep, and disrupted study sessions."

- "The Journal of American College Health published a survey stating that 73% of assailants and 55% of rape victims used drugs or alcohol prior to their assault."

*Source: College Binge Drinking (2006).

Financial problems have resulted from money spent on alcohol, which is more than is spent on books, soda, coffee, tea, juice, and milk combined (College Binge Drinking, 2006). The millions of alcoholics who are in recovery are examples of people who have taken initiative to make up for lost time and turn their lives around. After speaking with recovering alcoholics personally, they have indicated to me that alcohol has not helped their lives in any means, but certainly has shaped it. It taught them harsh lessons about experiencing "rock bottom" and the struggles to reclaim their lives — which they carry with them each day, one day at a time. They stated that if they could do it over again, they wouldn't have wasted precious years drinking. They would have chosen to pass a drink to someone else and never start. These individuals are the lucky ones — the survivors.

Over 100,000 people who die from alcohol-related incidents (accidents, cirrhosis of the liver) each year are unable to share their stories and wish they could have if they were alive (CDC, 2008).

The Governors spouses' initiative, *Leadership to Keep Children Alcohol Free,* was designed to make childhood drinking prevention a national health priority. This is a unique alliance of governors' spouses, federal agencies, and public and private organizations whose initiative is the only current national effort that specifically targets prevention of alcohol consumption in the 9 to 15-year-old age range (Leadership Overview, 2006).

Alcohol use by this cohort of children is an overlooked, yet very serious problem in the United States. Despite its known health and economic consequences, underage drinking still prevails. Unfortunately, the public is largely unaware both of the potentially harmful outcomes of early alcohol use and of large numbers of underage drinkers, especially younger ones.

The data on the onset of alcohol use at a young age is compelling and demonstrates the need for a prevention campaign (Leadership Overview, 2006).

- Approximately 18% of 8th-graders and 41% of 10th-graders have been drunk at least once.
- According to a recent survey, twice as many eighth-graders drink as use illegal drugs. About 76% more eighth-graders drink than smoke.

- Approximately 36% of ninth-graders report binge drinking in the past month.
- Among ninth-graders, girls consume alcohol and binge drink at rates almost equal to boys.

Research reveals that early alcohol use can have serious adverse consequences for mental, physical, and social development that may persist into adulthood. For example, research shows that 40% of individuals who begin drinking alcohol before age 13 manifest alcohol abuse or dependence at some point in their lives (Grant and Dawson, 1997).

The most recent studies indicate that alcohol may actually impair cognitive processes in young people, causing them to remember 10% less of what they learn than their non-drinking peers. Early alcohol use is often linked with poor school performance, depression, suicide, criminal and violent behavior, and risk-taking that can lead to serious injuries and death. Moreover, it can lead to premature sexual activity, with exposure to sexually transmitted diseases and/or resulting in unplanned teen pregnancies (Leadership Overview, 2006).

How can adults become actively involved in the prevention of youth drinking?

✓ Encourage conversation with a child. Demonstrate respect for a child's point of view and actively listen to her/him without interruption. The more you show respect for a child's viewpoint, the more likely a child will listen and respect your viewpoint. If there is something that is unpleasant to hear, refrain from outbursts of anger and take a few deep breaths to calm down and continue to listen.

✓ Talk to a child at an early age regularly about the use of alcohol and that actions have consequences. According to the U.S. Department of Health and Human Services, the average age when boys first try alcohol is 11-years-old and girls is 13-years-old (USDHHS, 2007). The earlier the addiction, without any early intervention, the more difficult it is to treat.

It is important to further mention that these actions can hurt many people that they would not intend on hurting.

✓ Teach a child about true friendship and how to stand up to troubling situations when peer pressure strikes.

✓ Discuss with an adolescent the effects of alcohol on the brain. Teens tend to take risks, explore, and ignore some of the messages from authority. Finding healthy ways to occupy their time that gives them a sense of purpose can make a positive difference in preventing youth drinking.

✓ Educational leaders should make available information about alcohol to all students. They should know the facts about underage drinking and propose realistic solutions to handle alcohol-related peer pressures.

✓ Educate children on how mass media sends messages about drinking alcohol. The message, "If you drink, your life will be better," needs to be properly addressed.

✓ Encourage a child to partake in positive extracurricular activities. The more active a child is, the less likely she/he is to engage in alcohol use (Hoffman, 2006).

✓ Parents should be involved in their child's life — setting rules for them to follow, monitoring their peer group closely, and looking for any warning signs of alcohol abuse such as a change in attitude, drop in grades, smell of alcohol on their breath, change in friends, withdrawal from family, and loss of money. Parents who drink influence their child's decisions. Studies show that teens are less likely to engage in drinking, if they know their parents are against it (NIAAA, 2006).

✓ Adults can become active in early prevention programs to reduce underage alcohol use (e.g. Mothers Against Drunk Driving (MADD)). Getting involved in alcohol policies on school campuses (especially in colleges/universities) and encouraging fraternities and sororities to sponsor alcohol-free events such as dances, sporting activities, movies, comedy nights, karaoke, live band performances, or public speaking events can help curb the use of alcohol.

Alcohol has become the unfortunate topic of discussion for many people's lives. It is important for youth to realize that there is much more to experience in life that is truly fulfilling than the consumption of alcohol. A child has complete capacity to make decisions to create her/his own life story that has meaning and lasting impact.

A useful website for locating an alcohol addiction treatment program is www.soberrecovery.com.

10.   SMOKING

Still a problem after all that we know?

Tobacco use is the leading cause of preventable death in the United States. It is responsible for nearly half a million deaths a year in the U.S. The tobacco industry has been largely successful in protecting their assets and continuing to distribute cigarettes to people throughout the world. After years of scientific studies proved the addictive nature of cigarettes, it is mind-boggling to imagine that this industry continues to boom. The tobacco products have been responsible for debilitating millions of people, causing various cardiovascular diseases and cancers (American Council on Science and Health, Inc., 2003).

For decades, the American Heart Association has worked to reduce the number of deaths and smoking-related diseases incurred by working with Congress to pass bills to have a smoke-free community. Many workplaces, schools, restaurants, and bars across the nation have banned smoking to promote clean indoor air. Many public places require people to go to a designated area, if they choose to smoke. Some communities are working to restrict smoking in the households and there are even towns that are going, to what many consider extreme measures, to ban smoking in the entire community and have only a few designated smoking areas. At the state, county, and municipal levels, there are discussions about increasing the excise tax on tobacco products in an effort to prevent and decrease purchases (American Council on Science and Health, Inc., 2003).

The 2004 National Survey on Drug Use and Health estimated over 70 million Americans aged 12 and older who reported currently using tobacco (NIDA, 2006):

- 60 million (nearly 25%) smoked cigarettes.
- 13.7 million (5.7%) smoked cigars.
- 7.2 million (3%) used smokeless tobacco.
- 1.8 million (0.8%) smoked pipes.

These statistics show how widely used tobacco is by today's youth. The National Institute on Drug Abuse (NIDA) has reported a significant decrease in the recent years in cigarette smoking. A recent quantitative analysis conducted through NIDA's Monitoring the Future Survey (2005) of eighth, tenth, and twelfth graders across the nation has shown over a 50% decrease in the use of tobacco products over the four plus decades and significant drops in the last decade.

The downhill trend in smoking

*From 1995 to 2005, there has been a decline in adolescents reported to smoke cigarettes:

8TH GRADERS

> ➢ 9.8% decrease (19.1% to 9.3%)

10TH GRADERS

> ➢ 13.0% decrease (27.9% to 14.9%)

12TH GRADERS

> ➢ 10.3% decrease (33.5% to 23.2%)

* Source: 2005 Monitoring the Future Survey. Reported cigarette use in past 30 days.

Why do kids smoke despite knowing the harmful effects?

So many teenagers smoke today and do not know why they started. Peer pressure from "the tribe" seems to be the greatest influence in why a child begins to smoke. Around 4,400 children become regular smokers each year. In fact, 90% of adult smokers started at or before the age of 19 (Kids and Smoking, 2007).

From an early age, children need to learn how to say "NO" to situations that they realize are bad. We must understand that it can be very difficult for a child to express her/his opinions freely to peers out of fear of rejection or humiliation, especially when she/he has to explain to a smoker who may already be addicted and get upset if a child does not conform. If a child isn't taught to say "NO," then it is much easier to lure her/him into the crowd by saying "Aw…come on."

Children must also be provided with alternative strategies for coping with peer pressure in various situations. Provided are advises for a child to tell her/his peers when confronted with the pressure to smoke:

"I am allergic to smoke. I get really sick any time I am near smoke and can throw up."

"The smoke will ruin my clothes and there is no way that I am going home smelling like smoke all over my body and hearing it from my parents."

"It will make my breath smell so bad and yellow my teeth. That is just disgusting!"

"No. That's o.k." (if the pressuring continues…) *"No thank you. You can do that, but I'll pass. I am not telling you what you have to do. Thank you, though."* (Then, a kid can change the theme confidently and quickly.)

Peer pressure is not the only factor involved in why a child decides to "light one up."

Other social factors that contribute to a child's decision to smoke include:

- Rebelling against authority.
- Doing something that is seen as forbidden in society.
- Curious about the taste.
- Wanting to be more adult-like.
- Parental role model provided as a smoker.
- Poor academic achievement.
- Media's portrayal of smoking as sexy and cool.

For those adolescents who smoke, adults should be aware that (USDHHS, 2004):

- One-third of young people experimenting with cigarettes become addicted by age 20.

- Cigarette addiction can lead to other forms of drug addiction (alcohol, substance abuse, prescription drugs, etc).

- Smokeless tobacco use is on the rise. One in five high school males uses spit tobacco.

In addition to the severe health effects that people are well aware of, here are some lifestyle consequences of smoking:

- Smoking controls how you plan your day. Needing to find a place to smoke all of the time becomes a priority versus enjoying time doing a healthy activity alone, with friends, and/or family.

- The amount of money wasted on cigarettes. A person who smokes one pack a day for ten years spends approximately $18,000-$20,000 that could be invested more intelligently.

- Smoking is a very important aspect of a smoker's life. Smoking largely determines a person's future social and family life — who one marries and is associated with.

- Smokers want to be mainly around other smokers. There is, often times, tension when a smoker is around a non-smoker for a certain time frame. If one decides to light up, a room becomes polluted for many non-smokers making it unfair for them to have to breathe in harmful chemicals.

- Most people do not want to be around smokers. The view of a smoker can be stigmatized as a dirty, smelly, low-class habit. There is a strong association that people have between education level and smoking — where the least educated smoke the most (Stellman and Resnicow, 1997).

- Word spreads very quickly about an individual's bad habits.

Relationships with others become affected. At the workplace this could cost an individual her/his job.

- Smoking poisons the body, especially affecting the skin, thereby causing wrinkles and accelerating aging (Murad, 2008).

- Smoking decreases lung functioning and the body becomes starved for oxygen. A smoker cannot physically keep up with a counterpart non-smoker, ultimately leading to a more sedentary lifestyle and not obtaining the proper amount of daily exercise.

- Smokers are more likely to start accidental fires than are non-smokers (Sacks and Nelson, 1994).

- Smoking is linked to erectile dysfunction in men, having a negative effect on one's sex life (Talking And Treating Erectile Dysfunction, 2009).

- Smoking can result in acquiring emphysema, which is an irreversible lung disease that can also damage one's heart. There is no cure for this disease once you get it. There is only prevention (USDHHS, 2004). DON'T SMOKE or STOP SMOKING IMMEDIATELY!

How to prevent children from smoking:

- As always…LEAD BY EXAMPLE! Don't smoke! If you do smoke and have a hard time in quitting, express to a child that you would have never started if you had known the addictive nature of cigarettes and that you don't want her/him having to deal with this problem. A child appreciates the truth and will be more apt to listen and follow an adult's advice. It would be best if you take the next step and quit smoking. A child will see the value in your words, along with your actions.

- Monitor peer groups and where a child plays regularly.

- Check for any unusual smells on clothes — whether there is cigarette smoke or a cover up fragrance. Immediately sit down and address the issue with a child. Smoking is a killer and if a child experiments with tobacco, an adult (most likely a parent) has to intervene before the addiction becomes worse.

- Teach the dangers of smoking to a child at an early age upon entering school. Discuss the risks associated with smoking cigarettes and using other tobacco-related products. Risks include ulcers, chronic bronchitis, heart disease, emphysema, stroke, lung cancer, and many other types of cancer.

- Discuss the addictive quality of nicotine and how people who quit have a very difficult time dealing with the psychological withdrawals including irritability, anxiety, sleep disturbances, nervousness, headaches, fatigue, nausea, and cravings for tobacco that can last days, weeks, months, years, or an entire lifetime.

- Don't expose a child to second hand smoke. Refrain from smoking in the house, in a car, or anywhere that a child is directly exposed to the smoke. This exposure can increase a child's chances of having ear infections, allergies, asthma, wheezing, pneumonia, and frequent upper respiratory tract infections.

- Express the negative effects that smoking has on a body. Show a child pictures or models of a smoker's lungs, as opposed to a pair of healthy lungs. Children understand the negative effect that smoking can have on their health. They sometimes need to see it up close to better understand it.

- Propose to children a visual that kissing a smoker is like kissing an ashtray. Children can make creative posters to demonstrate the unpleasant nature of smoking with its detriments and post them at their schools.

Additional information on this topic can be found at:
http://www.perkel.com/politics/issues/smoke.htm.

This is an excellent online resource for adults and youth addressing messages for teenagers about smoking cigarettes.   Author Marc Perkel relates to his audience in a very compelling, truthful manner discussing the reasons why young people should not smoke other than the fact that it will kill you. He shows youth how to use their brains in understanding the truth behind smoking and living life as an addict.

11.   CHILD ABDUCTION

Child abduction is one of the most common problems in our contemporary society.   Greater attention needs to be concentrated on studying this problem due to the severe consequences associated with this tragedy.   Several distinctive forms of child abduction (kidnapping) exist which include abduction by parents (most commonly) and abduction by strangers.

There are a host of factors that indicate why these actions occur. Strangers may have a desire to raise a child as her/his own, hold for ransom, abuse sexually, use for labor as a slave, and/or torture in other capacities.   On an average day, 91 children are reported missing every hour and a sexual predator will molest a child approximately 100 times before he (usually male) is arrested for the first time.   Many offenders (61%) did not report any history of child abuse.   Conversely, 26% accounted having experienced sexual abuse as a child (Morgan, 2009).

The Internet creates a new opportunity for lurking predators to solicit young boys and girls away from their homes to unfamiliar and dangerous ground.   These pedophiles are up on the latest fashion, music, hobbies, interests, and trends of today's youth.   They engage slowly or sometimes explicitly into sexually graphic conversations in order to lower their inhibitions and seduce them in order to meet them face-to-face.

Statistics on child abduction

* The latest statistics on child abduction, according to the United States Justice   Department, reveal some unsettling child abduction facts:

- On average, 2,185 children under the age of 18 were reported missing each day of the study year.
- This sums up to more than 800,000 children annually.
- Of that total, nearly 208,000, or about 25%, were family abductions.
- Someone other than a family member kidnapped an estimated 60,000.

- Of those abducted by someone other than a family member, 115 were not recovered safely or were killed.
- 60% of the kids who are kidnapped are murdered each year. Three quarters of them were killed within the first three hours.
- At the time of the latest study (in 2002), at least 322 children had been recovered safely through the AMBER Alert program.

* Source: http://www.life-prints.com/press-releases.htm (2008): Know your child abduction facts.

US Missing Children	Yearly	Daily
Total Reported Missing	806,000	2,208
Reported Abductions	354,400	907
Family Abductions	258,420	709
Non-Family Abductions	95,580	261

40% of All Children Abducted by Strangers are Killed

Source: www.amberready.com (2007): The Statistics Above are Provided by NCMEC and MACGLOCLEN on a 10 Year Average.

According to the National Household Surveys of Adult Caretakers and Youth (Hammer et al., 2002):

- 44% of family abducted children were younger than age six.
- 53% percent of family abducted children were abducted by their biological father and 25% were abducted by their biological mother.
- 46% percent of family abducted children were gone less than one week and 21% were gone one month or more.
- Only 6% of children abducted by a family member had not yet returned at the time of the survey interview.

Experts indicate that working quickly to distribute information about the kidnapped child is essential, as the first few hours of abduction are crucial. Note that 73% of all crimes against missing children occur within the first three hours and 99% take place within the first four hours. In August of 2004, AMBER alert safety centers were formed (in honor of Amber Hagerman, a 9-year-old girl who was kidnapped while riding her bicycle in Arlington, Texas and brutally murdered). The tragedy sparked an initiative to broadcast special "alerts" over the airwaves through a wide range of communication to inform law enforcement agencies and communities nationwide in a rapid-response effort to locate a missing child that is proposed to be seriously and truly missing. State-of-the-art child safety programs have been developed to better equip a child and parents with the necessary tools to combat these abductions (AMBER Ready, 2007).

The most recent inventions to protect from abductions

Various wireless safety programs have been created that allow parents to store valuable information about their child including videos, identity information, pictures, and optional fingerprints to aid a child's recovery. A sample of DNA from a child's saliva can be stored at room temperature and can be used to build a genetic profile if the child went missing. Law enforcement agencies are able to transmit information from a parent's wireless phone to police headquarters greatly increasing the speed of recovery (AMBER Alert, 2007).

To prevent from abductions, a secret device has been created that is discreetly placed on a child. Young boys and girls across America are becoming educated on how to properly utilize this gadget in the case of a real emergency. Police stations are tuned in to this device that serves as a global positioning system to immediately locate a missing child's whereabouts. Child Abduction Response Teams (CARTs) respond swiftly to incidents of missing and abducted children. The teams include regional law enforcement investigators, forensic experts, AMBER Alert coordinators, search and rescue professionals, policy makers, crime intelligence analysts, victim service providers, and other interagency resources. Phone companies across the nation are cooperating to be a part of this revolutionary concept to help eliminate kidnappings in the United States (AMBER Alert, 2007).

Safety tips for parents to prevent their child from being abducted:

- First and foremost, keep all lines of communication open with your child. Convey messages of love, respect, and understanding. A child must feel safe to come to a parent regarding any and all concerns in life.

- Raise a child with a strong sense of self-respect. Predators long for children lacking self-esteem and feeling lonely — craving attention any way they can get it.

- Talk to your child about sex and disclose the topic of sexual predators. Naive children are perfect prey for kidnappers.

- Know your child's specific whereabouts and the company she/he is in. A cell phone is a tremendous tool that can be used for communication, especially in the case of emergencies.

- Stranger danger is a very important concept for young boys and girls to understand. A child as young as 2-years-old should know her/his parents' names and be able to speak them to someone in order to get help if ever separated. Parents should educate young children on who they are allowed to communicate with.

- Teach your child that safety is the most important thing in the world. Emphasize the importance of her/him never telling anyone that she/he is home alone and to never open the door for strangers. A wise option is to prohibit a child from answering the phone or the door if it rings. Parents should ensure that a child knows how to dial 911 in the case of an emergency.

- If you and your child become separated in a large area such as a grocery store, shopping mall, or busy area with many people, there should be a plan put into place to reunite. Children should either stay put the moment they realize that they are separated from their family or meet in a common area in the place — that should be immediately assigned upon entering in the case of a separation. Predators look for opportunities of wandering children looking for their mommy and daddy. They pose as police officers or helpful adults that "know where their parents are" and will bring the child to them safely.

- You should carry a recent, clear photo of your child for identification purposes.

- In the case of your child being in imminent danger, have a code word that symbolizes that she/he is in danger. This can be relayed through text and/or voicemail using wireless forms of communication.

- Avoid the term, "Don't talk to strangers!" Refrain from teaching confusing messages to your child. Over half of the time, the abductor is someone that the child may know or at least be familiar with. It is a stranger who may actually be able to save a child's life. Rather, educate a child on potentially dangerous situations, how to best avoid them, and how to react if the situation occurs. Practicing to role-play situations is a great visual helping a child best remember how to reenact a similar situation involving danger, most effectively.

- Teach a child what to do in the case of an actual attempted abduction into a car. Educate a child to first attempt to run as fast and far away as possible screaming for help. If they are being wrestled into the car, teach them how to kick, punch, bite, etc. A quick kick to the shin followed by a sharp blow to the groin area buys time to loosen a predator's grip. Open hand strikes between the eyes can temporarily stun an individual and allow for escape.

If a child is captured and trapped in the front seat with a stranger, here are some options for escape (Exley, 2003):

- Remain calm and wait for the driver to approach a stoplight, stop sign, or encounter traffic. Fall onto the driver's lap and press hard on the gas pedal to cause an accident while protecting the head. This will help draw attention to the situation.

- Falling onto the lap of the driver at a stopped moment and slamming on the horn, yelling for help, and demonstrating concern through body language can get others' attention. It is best for a child not to panic, but to wait for moments when the car is stopped and do everything possible before they get out of sight from people where no one can help.

- If the driver gets out of the car for whatever reason with the keys and locks the car with the kidnapped child inside, advise for the child to first try pressing the horn, looking for others for help, or opening the door somehow. If this does not work, inserting something small into the ignition key such as a button can prevent the car from starting. If the child cannot find anything, then attempting to break the gearshift by leaning on it is another option. The best bet is to try to get out of the car and reach for help.

If a child is trapped in the trunk of a car, here are some options for her/him to get someone's attention (Exley, 2003):

- Pull at wires that lead to the taillights. This will disrupt the brake lights and alert drivers that there is a problem and hopefully they will contact the authorities for help.

- Tear at the rubber sealing that separates between the trunk lid and the back of the car. There may be enough space to get a hand out to wave back and forth forewarning drivers that there is someone in the trunk.

- Listen and try to sense when the car comes to a stop and then kick the trunk lid as hard as possible to alert drivers behind that there is a problem.

If a child is trapped in a strange house or room and cannot escape (doors/windows locked and bars are up on windows), here are some options to get attention:

- Leave a trail of evidence to get someone's attention such as hair, pieces of skin, articles of clothing, messages in walls, etc.

- Take a sock, towel, or some piece of clothing and roll it into a ball stuffing it into the toilet to clog it.   Flush repeatedly to cause it to overflow. A maintenance worker will need to be contacted or if on a second floor or higher, the water can seep onto the below ceiling and hopefully people below will notice quickly and alert maintenance of the problem.

If children were more aware of tricks that predators use to lure them away and techniques on how to escape danger, then the number of kidnappings and murders would drastically decrease. Both children and adults need to prepare child abduction prevention and emergency plans in the event of an actual abduction. When a child is missing, seconds become the difference between life and death.

12.   HOMOPHOBIA

"That dude's a fag!" "Are you in or out?" "Let's set this boy straight!" "Why are you so gay?" These aforementioned statements are heard among today's youth and unfortunately are spoken more than ever. Do kids really know what they are saying when they say these statements or ask these questions? Do they really mean it?

There is a lack of consistency between homophobia being a true phobia. A phobia, by definition, is "an intense, illogical or abnormal fear of a specified thing" (Webster's, 1999). The fear is usually excessive, often times unreasonable, and those who possess a particular phobia usually avoid it. Most people who have phobias recognize that they have this fear and are inspired to change a behavior to overcome it. The homophobic individual possesses a wide variety of negative emotions toward homosexual people. These people do not try to avoid gays, but instead display hostility and aggression. They do not consider themselves to have any problem and do not see a need to change their attitude.

Homophobia is certainly a source of much violence in our society. The homophobic person takes on an extreme role as the heterosexual to prove that she/he is not gay. This usually occurs more commonly with males, rather than females, and that is where the homophobic man's actions can become violent (Gilligan, 2001).

They take on the extreme masculine gender role in situations and avoid displaying feminine stereotypical qualities of being loving, caring, understanding, nurturing, intimate, passionate, and displaying emotions of vulnerability such as sadness, fear, or depression. Rather, these individuals display a feeling that many violent men let themselves feel and that is anger — which often results in hostile takeovers. This feeling of being "a man" can set the ego into full gear and result in sexual promiscuity where the domineering male has to be in control and often times in complete control of the girl, resulting in potentially harmful physical and mental abuse — if not rape and murder (Gilligan, 2001).

Masculinity: what it means to be a man according to society

Let us first take a look at the notion at what it means to be "a man." Manhood is a term that has been socially constructed since a society of men first existed interacting in the marketplace, competing for resources, and acquiring tangible goods as evidence of success. Masculinity is measured by power, success, wealth, and status. Within the dominant society, individuals who are white, middle class, early to middle-aged, and heterosexual men define masculinity. This sociological phenomenon of manhood takes a step further to exclude and devalue other groups of people that are not within that classification such as women, non-white men, non-native born men, and homosexuals (Kimmel, 1994).

What are so many men afraid of when they encounter those "other" men that come off as effeminate in the way they carry themselves? A boy's first role model of what it means to be a man comes from his father. According to the social learning theory model, children become "gendered" learning how to behave as boys or girls through observation and imitation (Bandura and Walters, 1963).

For instance, a boy observes how his father behaves with his mother in various situations. Also, the tone of a father's voice used in reprimanding a son versus a daughter displays an early-learned behavior of "being a man" and that is aggression. A boy often observes that a father is away from home sending the message that they are breadwinners of a family (Benokraitis, 2008).

During the socialization process, children learn what behavior is appropriate for a certain gender (Davies, 2002). "Gendering" takes place consciously and unconsciously in all aspects of society where our perceptions and behaviors towards individuals are adjusted based on age, gender, race, ethnicity, etc. Examples include teachers in the way they behave with boys versus girls each day, friends in how they play games and socialize, the clothes young people wear, the competitive and aggressive nature of activities performed, and the images of celebrities portrayed in the media.

The secret reason for why homophobia exists

What our society calls manhood is merely a fear barrier. Homophobia is more than simply the fear of homosexuals. The secret of manhood lies in the fear of OTHER MEN. Homophobia is the fear that other men will "unmask us" and "reveal us to the world" —

that we do not measure up to the ideals that society has created as to what it means to be a man (Kimmel, 1994).

Homophobia is a "central organizing principle of our cultural definition of manhood" (Kimmel, 1994: 8). Saying, "You are gay!" in essence is saying, "You are not a real man! You are weak! You are not valued! You are powerless! You are unworthy!" This fear is the fear of being humiliated and to be made to feel inadequate. We are ashamed to be afraid and this results in silence, especially when sexist or "gay-bashing jokes" take place (Kimmel, 1994). As long as this silence exists in "manhood," homophobia will pervade the world and cause harm to innocent individuals beyond measure.

Hurting anyone deliberately based on their sex, race, creed, ethnicity, sexual preference, and socioeconomic class is unfair and downright cruel. Among the general public, a double standard for this and other social issues exists. We hear people say that they have nothing against gays or that they have no hatred toward people of different color and that they are very "tolerant people." What is the TRUTH about how people REALLY feel?

How do the following statements make you feel?

"I have nothing against homosexuals, I just don't believe that they should have the right to get married. I certainly wouldn't want my kid to be gay."

"I have nothing against people of different color, I just don't want my child marrying anyone of that race. I have nothing against the individual, though."

"I have nothing against people of that ethnic background. I just don't want to be friends or have personal contact with someone of that background."

"I have no hatred toward women at all. I just don't feel like they should be given the chance to run our country or big businesses."

Do any of those statements pose a hidden truth about how you truly feel? Do you feel ashamed to feel this way or do you justify your actions with "proof" that "these kind of people" are bad and do not deserve what "other people" deserve? If so, please re-read this section carefully and understand that this is a centralized principle in our society, especially among men and in order to reverse this problem, we need to hammer at the root of this issue. Any unwillingness to rewrite the misperceptions that you or someone you may know has had since childhood about homophobia cannot only be costly for our society's future, but detrimental for your own or someone else's self-development and must be turned around.

Consequences of homophobia

Many homosexual individuals suffer from daily emotional, psychological, and physical batter from many different sources. Not only do they receive ridicule and violence from their peers, but also live with the fear of rejection from their parents if they divulge their sexuality. Most religious conservatives hold the belief that homosexuality is "abnormal, unnatural, and a mental disease" (Robinson, 2006). These factors contribute to why the suicide rate among gays and lesbians is so towering. According to the U.S. Health and Human Services (1989):

> *"Gay adolescents were two to three times more likely than peers to attempt suicide, accounting for as many as 30% of completed youth suicides each year.... 26% percent of gay youth are forced to leave home because of conflicts with their families over their sexual identities. Up to half engage in prostitution to support themselves, greatly increasing their risk for HIV infection."*

What must become evident from the above statistics is that the culture's homophobia can lead to a host of problems that target today's society including:

- Suicide,
- Depression,
- Violence,
- STDs,
- Drug addictions,
- Prostitution,
- Life of crime,

- Being homeless,
- Low self-esteem and needing to hate other groups of people,
- Intolerance,
- Other health-related problems.

Strategies to provide children who encounter uncomfortable situations involving homophobia:

- If a child is called "gay," "faggot," "homo," or any other derogatory name, have a child simply ignore it and let it go, rather than make a big deal of the matter. Most likely, a verbal attacker just wants negative attention and does not mean what she/he says and it will pass. If a child feels more comfortable to smile and laugh it off, then that is also fine as long as the problem does not persist.

- If a bully continues with this name calling, proceed to ask her/him, "What is your point? For what reason are you calling me names like that? Are you afraid of something?"

- If a bully states, "I can call you whatever I feel like calling you," or "I say you are gay because you act like it," then the victim can respond with, "You are so immature and annoying, but thanks for the compliment." Then, as hard as it may be or as hurt as a child may feel, she/he should not feel threatened by the bully, but rather commit to ignore the person or tell a teacher or a close friend, privately. A child should not continue to engage in any conversation having to prove she/he is not gay. This is how other problems arise from just a few "simple words" spoken.

- Have a child speak to a guidance counselor at school if she/he knows of anyone else being "bashed" or inappropriately teased.

- Have a child speak with an authority figure at school in regards to any plots that are being developed to hurt a specific group of people based on their unique attributes.

- If you are a parent, be cognizant of the messages that you provide your children each day about gender expectations. Teach tolerance toward all groups of individuals from all different backgrounds.

What to do for a parent if a child is homosexual

- You may be in shock when the news is broken to you, but keep cool and allow a child to fully display her/his feelings. A child needs to feel safe when expressing emotions to loved ones.

- Throw away any prejudices that you may have about gays, lesbians, or bisexuals and accept your child for who she/he is. No one wants to feel rejected, especially by one's parents.

- Continue to provide unconditional love to your child. Convey to a child that hearing this news about sexuality does not change how you feel about her/him.

- Refrain from treating your child any differently than you normally would. Remember that your child is still the same multi-faceted individual — despite expressing her/his sexuality.

- It is important to realize that you cannot change your child's sexual orientation. You can educate yourself on how homosexual individuals feel and what they experience — to better understand your child.

- Remind your child that you love her/him so much and that you are always there for support. It is important for homosexual individuals to love who they are and not feel that they have to live a lie and be someone they are not — carrying a tremendous burden of guilt and shame (Bidstrup, 2002).

The solution for homophobia lies in "root education" where we understand and address the origin of the problem and work from there. Any form of organized resistance against or outward promotion of homophobia, such as having gay parades or political activist events, must discontinue so we can prevent a recurrence of this insidious problem. These events reinforce stereotypes that we are trying to dismiss in society.

People should be tolerant to homosexuals and treat them with respect and understanding. "Otherness" should not become a fear and the root of hatred. Homosexuality must not be promoted at schools and/or media outlets, otherwise it can become a new wave of fashion for young children who are vulnerable and they will internalize what is popular. In this way, children may understand homosexuality as a new, desirable trend.

13. VIOLENCE

"If he could only ride his bike up the road and hang out with the rest of us, we would have accepted him." "If he'd go behind the church and just try it with us, then he wouldn't single himself out." "If he'd only dress with style, then he wouldn't be picked on." "He has never had a girlfriend. I wonder about him." I recall those very same statements spoken to me during my youth. Staying true to oneself often results in isolation — feeling alone, not due to choice, but due to a crucifixion of words and actions imparted by those in one's microcosmic world. Violence in society comes in many forms with a wide variety of consequences. Throughout this topic, the main factors associated with violence are addressed with proposed solutions.

Contributing factors to violence that are discussed:

- BULLYING
- DISCRIMINATION
- FEELINGS OF SHAME
- INCREASED EXPOSURE TO VIOLENCE THROUGH MASS MEDIA
- TECHNOLOGY & INTERNET SAFETY CONCERNS
- FAMILY & INTERPERSONAL ISSUES
- EFFECT OF IMPRISONMENT

Children and bullying

Bullying is the most common thing that most children experience to some degree, in one form or another. The fear of being asked or told to do something when you do not feel comfortable doing it can pose a serious threat, or so one thinks, to a child's acceptance among peers. A child may feel that if she/he does not follow the crowd and do what everyone else does, then she/he will not be accepted and won't have friends. The topic of bullying is one of my specialties from first-hand experience and I can profoundly state that "being popular" at school is a misguided perception.

What is popularity anyway? The guidelines on that are often dictated by a group of closed-minded individuals that consider themselves superior to others for whatever reason. When in essence, the true testament of being popular is the universal respect by all individuals and how one truly values people and accepts them for who they are.

As it presently stands, bullying is still common among children and often times, one either takes on a role as the victim or the bully. The effects from long-term bullying can be quite pervasive on the victim throughout all aspects of her/his life impacting social well-being, along with self-confidence, as well as on the aggressor who may go on to engage in more serious antisocial behaviors. We have seen and heard about issues including bomb threats to blow up schools, guns being found in student lockers, and unfortunate school shootings claiming innocent lives. Many times, individuals involved in conspiring or committing these actions are bullied victims or misunderstood outcasts who equated justice with revenge on their tormenters.

Tolerance for one another is necessary and encouragement should be the foundation for how we treat others. Children must understand that no one likes to feel less than anyone, hurt, or misunderstood. Everyone wishes to be a shining star in some way and the fact of the matter is that people from all walks of life have to find what makes them unique and feel valued. Parents and teachers may or may not tell their children or students how special they are, but it does mean a lot to a child to receive these empowering words of praise and encouragement from time-to-time.

Bullying can take on many forms from public humiliation, embarrassment, rumors, verbal harassment, online harassment, and/or physical abuse. These individuals that feed off of others like blood-sucking parasites desire wrong kinds of attention and this marks a lacking of something in their lives. They target others that are either insecure, shy, already not accepted by others, or just isolated and unwilling to stand up for themselves. A child's power, as an individual, is far greater than what she/he may think. Standing up for others and not feeling bad about the outcome of how she/he appears to others, exude strength. In turn, the depth of character will be noticed over time.

How does a child stop the bullying?

Tips that adults can suggest to children dealing with this issue:

- Be understanding that bullies are the exception in the world and lack an emotional intelligence that you have.

- Work with your friends to help you distract bullies from their cruelty.

- Refrain from fueling any negativity personally directed. Do not overreact and feed in to the bullying by responding to unkind words spoken or by asking them to fight; quite often all that they want is to be heard. Hear it and dismiss it.

- Act respectful to all people, including bullies, and do not gossip about others.

- Be humble and laugh. Do not be so serious or tell everyone that you are the best and brag about it. Getting the last word is not always the best solution.

- If all else fails, a child should tell an adult who has authority to support the bullied individual. A bully can be punished by law; it is a crime!

Throughout my childhood, I was educated first hand on the term: BULLYING. I experienced being singled out in a variety of cruel and mean ways. I can state candidly that my time around peers could be portrayed as a scene of great humiliation, confusion, and disrespect. Daily strength, stability, courage, and love provided at home from my family members and at school by my teachers, reinforced my self-worth and values. Growing up, I endured what so many other children go through on a day-to-day basis. The concern lies in what today's youth feel inside and receives for messages from adults.

Violence at schools

A school environment is where children learn to a large extent what society is all about. This is a time where children learn about gender roles and identities and begin to form their own opinions on what is acceptable. They develop their own social and personal identities. Schools are intended to be safe places for learning, but as we know it is, often times, the site of violent behaviors — resulting in much physical and mental abuse. There are daily occurrences where kids in high school are "coming out of the closet" and then being called horrible names or worse yet — physically beaten up at school.

How is all of this happening in such a "safe, learning environment?" What role do policymakers, administrators, teachers, and other adult figures have in preventing violence at our schools? Policymakers are working on protecting learners from discriminations and various hate crimes (hazing, bullying in all of its forms), but offensive behaviors such as shoving someone's books out of their hands in the hall, swearing or saying racial slurs, and "initiating" new team members in the locker room have taken place for years and continue to do so.

Has this been an unconscious acceptance as "kids being kids?" Do administrators and teachers turn their backs on the fundamental core issues of today's society due to a fear of parental retaliation, being physically hurt, and/or a loss of their job? What real plans are put into place for preventing violence in our schools and appropriately handling it, if it occurs?

The stories of devastating violent killings that have taken place at schools dating back to the University of Texas shootings in 1966, the Pearl High School shootings in 1997, the Columbine High School shootings in 1999, the Amish school shootings in 2006, the Virginia Tech University shootings in 2007, and the Winnenden school shootings in Germany in 2009 have shown the devastating effects that have taken place as a result of chronic bullying. These were unfortunate happenings that should be, but were not prevented. Could these tragedies have been prevented? If so, how?

"I am not insane, I am angry. I killed because people like me are mistreated every day. I did this to show society, push us and we will push back. All throughout my life, I was ridiculed, always beaten, always hated. Can you, society, truly blame me for what I do? Yes, you will. It was not a cry for attention. It was not a cry for help. It was a scream in sheer agony saying that if you can't pry your eyes open, if I can't do it through pacifism,

if I can't show you through the displaying of intelligence, then I will do it with a bullet."

-Luke Woodham, student gunman at Pearl High School

Extensive harassment has been the reason for much of these tragedies that have resulted in lives lost in a school setting. This means both homicide and self-inflicted violence — resulting in suicide. If one stands out as a little different, then peers can make another student's life a living hell. So what can we expect from those chronically bullied? Can we blame them for such retaliation toward society?

Virginia Tech University tragedy

"You had a hundred billion chances and ways to have avoided today, but you decided to spill my blood. You forced me into a corner and gave me only one option. The decision was yours. Now you have blood on your hands that will never wash off."

-Seung-Hui Cho, 23-year old Virginia Tech gunman

What can explain the reason why one young individual could go on a shooting spree resulting in the worst shooting rampage in modern U.S. history killing 33 students and professors, including himself. Who is to take the blame for such a horrific undertaking? Of course Seung-Hui Cho is to blame for his decisions made, but looking further, we find society and the influence of popular culture cleverly pussyfooting into the souls of youth.

Cho was raised in suburban Washington D.C. where his parents worked at a dry cleaners place. Read from his manifesto left in his dorm room at the University, details describing him as "anti-woman" and "anti-rich kids" and that he was against "debauchery" and "deceitful charlatans." His note was several pages long and explained his actions stating, "You caused me to do this." This statement is similar in citing the reasons for the killings to Woodham's statement when he was personally interviewed by the Secret Service saying, "People always picked on me and they always called me gay or stupid stuff like that" (Lagorio, 2007).

Warning signs leading to the Virginia Tech massacre (Apuzzo, 2007):

➢ Cho was cited as very shy, insecure, and a loner by his teachers at school.

➢ His classmates cited him as severely picked on for much of his school life.

➢ He put a question mark representing his name on a sign in sheet for class.

➢ Over a year prior to the shootings, Cho was said to have been harassing two women with unwanted messages and was taken to a psychiatric hospital. He was declared as a danger to himself after a psychiatric assessment.

➢ Cho was referred to the university's disciplinary system as a result of the stalking incidents.

➢ He wrote twisted, creative obscenity and violence-filled screenplays fantasizing about stalking and killing a teacher who sexually molested them and using a wide variety of weapons that former classmates claimed they would not have even thought.

➢ He was removed from an English class and referred to the university's counseling service.

➢ He was said to be taking antidepressants.

Why then with all of the warning signs present over the years was this not prevented? Why did someone not take a stand and strongly intervene to save lives? Whose responsibility is it to step in to help? It is true that behaviors of this nature should trigger a response to intercede from authority members. Cho's actions along with the Columbine shooters displayed out of the ordinary behavior, but these aberrant behaviors have become all too common among teenagers and young adults. And why is this so? Take a look outside of our bodies and the answers can be found in the world that we are living, in which today's young people are constantly polluted with toxicity from lyrics in music and where the top-grossing films are laced with vulgar comedy and gun violence. Many best selling books are ridden with violence and bloodshed. Cleaning up the mess that has been made is a process that adults have started and are responsible for ending.

Identifying these school shooters over the years as simply "deranged," and blaming loose regulations for allowing student acceptance into university and acquisition of guns, addresses the mere surface of a much deeper concern that we may not be willing to face — SOCIETY'S WILLINGNESS FOR TOLERANCE — to be able to accept all people from all backgrounds in all capacities.

I agree that there should be sound safety measures taken to ensure that all students in schools are protected, especially at open campuses at colleges and universities. It is important for everybody to learn from these tragic events and improve securities and communications at our schools.

Proposed plans to consider:

- Better identify students with mental health issues and provide the help they need.

- Be on high alert for copycat acts of violence in weeks following a school shooting, during this "higher risk zone."

- Review and reevaluate current emergency and preparedness programs.

- Have panic alarms in all buildings throughout all campuses.

- Have a 24-hour a day secured residence hall with physical security and visible human security.

- Have emergency blue phones where people can press a button and receive help immediately.

- Have emergency 911 calls diverted directly to the university dispatch center.

- Have emergency messages given to the cell phones of students.

- Have increased school securities with more law enforcement present on site.

"They were tired of those who were insulting them, harassing them. They weren't going to take this anymore and they wanted to stop it. Unfortunately, that's exactly what they did."

-Eric Veik, friend of Harris and Klebold, the two shooters at Columbine

It was stated that the two killers in the Columbine High School massacre in May 1999 were subjected to repeated public humiliation, name-calling, insults, rejection, accusations of being homosexuals, and physical abuse. These allegations were confirmed by many of the students, especially the "jocks" who often tormented the two (Gilligan, 2001). What was it that caused Harris and Klebold to retaliate with such violent behaviors, considering the fact that teasing and bullying take place quite often within our schools each day and it rarely ends up with someone being killed?

Eric Harris has been deemed "textbook psychopathic" in his actions, which indicates that he had complete awareness of his actions and was quite rational. Degrading messages on his website about the human race are indicative of someone with a superiority complex out to punish everyone in society for being inferior. His actions toward others are without feeling and grasping another's emotions. The true psychopathic individual fails to understand emotions such as love, hate, or fear because she/he did not experience them directly (Cullen, 2007).

Feelings of shame

The risk factors associated with violence have been so often studied, but major questions still remain. Is violence more prevalent among people of a certain age, race, ethnicity, religion, gender, or socioeconomic background? Violence is multi-factored and is a result of biological, environmental, and psychological actions. It is evident that all individuals from any particular group are not violent (Gilligan, 2001).

Certain variables can be shown to have the effect of increasing or decreasing the frequency and severity of violence, but it has been examined that shame is a necessary cause of violence. The probability that individuals will demonstrate violence when exposed to poverty and/or discrimination of some sort for a prolonged period increases due to the higher percentage of those being subjected to feelings of shame and their perception that there is no escape from it — except by violent action (Gilligan, 2003).

We can understand how most violent and hostile incidents commonly reflect the hatred that select people have toward other people that fall outside of the boundaries that are acceptable — as it pertains to one's socioeconomic background, sexuality, religion, race, ethnicity, beliefs, and how these may (or may not) differ from one's own feelings. Most school attacks come from "loners" or "outcasts" who felt bullied or persecuted by others.

Peers indicated that the two assailants, Harris and Klebold, felt that their peers were attacking their masculinity by calling them "gay" or "faggot" and they were made fun of because they didn't have sexual experiences. What is also evident is that their perception of how their peers viewed them was of disrespect, whether or not it is completely justified is up for debate. Their mental reaction to those events was of feeling shame and they wanted to replace that feeling with one of respect and the only way they believed this could be achieved was through an act of rage and destruction (Gilligan, 2001). It must be known that by reducing these shame-provoking inequities in social and economic status, the public health of today's society will be increased.

This excerpt was written in the *New York Times* (May 1999) and was taken from the website of Eric Harris:

"God I can't wait till I kill you people. I'll just go to some downtown area and blow up and shoot everything I can. Feel no remorse, no sense of shame. I don't care if I live or die in the shootout, all I want to do is kill and injure as many of you as possible."

Seung-Hui Cho was said to be on antidepressants to provide him with a more assertiveness in his attitude and emotional needs. It was said that he would gain the nerve to talk to girls that he liked at the university but only to result in further rejection and labeled a stalker. After years of abuse from his peers dating back to middle school, Cho had carried such a feeling of anger and deep rage with him daily. From there, he turned his emotions into an outcry toward humanity (Baxter, 2007). Quite possibly, his shame and frustration in seeing that still nothing has changed in experiencing rejections and being outcast (unable to fit in) caused him to be heard a different way. His feelings are clearly explained below.

"You have vandalized my heart, raped my soul, and torched my conscience. You thought it was one pathetic boy's life you were extinguishing. Thanks to you, I die like Jesus Christ, to inspire generations of the weak and the defenseless people."

Let's challenge violence and put a stop to it!

Strategies for educators to overcome violence within schools:

- Embed these taboo topics into the curriculum. Fear is a state of mind for people due to a lack of understanding and education about the topic. Address topics of tolerance, discrimination, hate crimes, and media literacy directly and discuss violence in all of its forms and how to prevent it.

- Educators have a responsibility to be role models and demonstrate diversity, equality, and tolerance for all people through their actions. Offer workshops to educators on the topics of violence and bullying.

- Promote diversity and human rights by having banners,

collages, posters, and/or other types of media displayed throughout schools.

- Facilitate emotions of equality within classrooms and throughout the school. The existence of inequality brings about levels, which can result in competition for status to not feel inferior. This inequality stimulates shame and shame stimulates violence.

- Allow children to openly discuss their feelings with adult figures without fear of punishment or social embarrassment. Point out to children that they are not crazy for having thoughts of anger, rage, and depression. Help them figure out why they feel a certain way and discuss strategies to help them overcome these emotions so they feel better.

- Address any violent situation as quickly as possible to restore order. Be strong and show that this behavior is not tolerated.

- Administrators and various teacher representatives throughout a school can meet regularly to develop behavior expectations for a school community. Putting forth a standard that is agreed upon and able to be upheld by adults at school is a great foundation for learning in a safe environment.

- Hire hall monitors who reinforce school policy and stand patrol (with a smile and not looking for trouble, specifically). Expecting teachers to always be in the halls between classes and monitoring behavior is unrealistic and unfair for those preparing and closing up classes. Lack of money in the budget should not be an excuse for lacking the assurance of safety and enforcement of school rules that a good hall monitor can serve.

- Have a school resource officer in the building as a helpful figure to children and adults. She/he can provide meaningful discussions in a classroom and help formulate a safe, positive climate for adults and children at school.

- Propose the idea to implement school uniforms being worn on a regular basis. This would help eliminate the competition for best style. Instituting this policy has many advantages including an improved scholastic performance, student security, student discipline, and school morale.

Violent tendencies begin quite young and there are many factors that have been proposed that contribute to a person becoming violent including having violent parents, watching violent shows on television, playing violent video games with lewd or crude themes, listening to music with violent lyrics, demonstrating cruelty to animals, living in a violent neighborhood, and being predisposed genetically from birth. Having these factors do not guarantee that one will become a juvenile delinquent and grow up to be an aggressive person by any means, but the odds are largely against her/him. One must realize what can contribute to the violence problem in society and then changes can be made to one's lifestyle to position away from these inclinations.

When someone feels rejected, shamed, or does not feel accepted, there are choices to be made about how to handle the situation. Often times, children and adults resort to violence as an outlet to be heard. They see their role models in the music industry or a sporting arena display such behaviors and feel that it must be all right to do the same, since they are idealized celebrities making a lot of money.

Mass media and its influence on violence

The average American child will have watched 100,000 acts of televised violence, including 8000 depictions of murder by the time she/he is in sixth grade (Children and television violence, 2005). Viewing wrestling matches, boxing events, war movies, "mature" cartoons, and other violent situations on television and the silver screen may seem entertaining. However, it is important for children and adults to realize that these are strictly forms of entertainment not intended to be re-created by anyone and should not be taken any further. Some young people cross that line and their curiosity gets the best of them. Backyard wrestling matches and street fighting activities can result in broken bones, paralysis of the body, and/or a criminal record.

Messages condoning violence are sent to children through mass media in all forms every day. An overwhelming amount of research has supported the notion that constant exposure to violence stimulates hostile behavior. For instance, violent films comprise over 60% of all films released (Children and television violence, 2005).

Many video games today are so visually graphic and real life that a person can go on a virtual killing spree and experience feelings of violence. When the release of a new video game entertainment system took place in November 2006, it caused pandemonium outside of stores throughout the United States. There were reports of attempted robberies where people were demanding money from others waiting in line. In Connecticut, one man was shot and wounded. The crowds in a California Wal-Mart store became so unruly pushing and shoving one another that they had to contact police authorities and shut down the store. On Black Friday in 2008, a Wal-Mart employee was trampled to death by a stampede in Valley Stream, New York (Hsu, 2008).

It is important to realize that not every violent action portrayed in the media sparks a violent response. The depiction of violence as entertainment (drama) rather than as tragedy triggers violent behavior. Violence in television programming became a serious issue in the 1970s. With the deregulation of children's programming and the advent of the VCR in the 1980s, children were able to view once restricted shows more readily and frequently. In the U.S., there has always been a steadfast mentality to prevent government intervention in media operations proclaiming that it would violate the First Amendment of the Constitution ensuring freedom of speech and freedom of the press (Government and Industry Responses to Media Violence, 2009).

As media times progressed in the 1990s and shows displaying violence became more popular, Canada, the United Kingdom, Australia, Norway, Sweden, and many European countries stated that any enterprise using public airwaves must be "socially responsible." The federal broadcast regulator, the Canadian Radio-television and Telecommunications Commission (CRTC), began one of the first initiatives to help families deal with television violence. The commission met with public health professionals, educators, policymakers, consumer groups, and cable and program production industries. After 1.3 million Canadians petitioned against media violence, and this proposed policy was approved by the prime minister, all privately owned and conventional television networks were to follow a code. This launched the creation of similar codes by other specialty and pay-TV services (Government and Industry Responses to Media Violence, 2009).

*The Code's provisions included:

- "A prohibition on airing programs that are gratuitously violent and that promote or glamorize violent acts."
- "A promise to develop a program classification system."
- "A commitment to sensitivity about violence against vulnerable groups, such as women and minorities."
- "A statement that violence would not be shown as a preferred way of solving problems, or as the central theme of children's programming and that children's programming would not invite dangerous imitation."

*Source: Government and Industry Responses to Media Violence (2009).

The dilemma became more difficult as it pertained to government intervention of censorship on various programming. In 1994, the creation of the "V chip" was used as a resource for parents to control a child's exposure to violent television programs. Also, there were classification systems being given for many programs, but not all, displaying an age-appropriate rating and a content-based rating to help parents regulate what should and should not be viewed by children (Jordan, 2008). Notice, these interventions were put forth to help prevent children from being exposed to violent nature in the media, especially the most vulnerable children who didn't have parents that took care to monitor their television viewings.

Technology and Internet safety

Technology has brought about enormous strides in our understanding of the world where we can take virtual trips to just about anywhere. We can go shopping, take virtual field trips, watch movies, listen to music downloads, pay bills, play video games, and chat with people across the world all while sitting at home. Major problems have arisen since the turn of the century involving the worldwide globalization of an unregulated media that was unheard of in the past. Children are able to access virtually anything with the click of a mouse and this poses challenges to former protection strategies in years passed. A person from one side of the world can talk to another person in chat rooms and community forums.

There are various popular social networking websites where one has the ability to broadcast herself/himself in a not so educational light. Children can easily videotape random acts of violence onto their cell phones or digital cameras and upload them onto the Internet. This opens the door for many potential problems, mainly inviting wrong crowds unknowingly viewing the scene and inviting possibilities for communication with strangers.

Children often visit chat rooms to "meet people" and "get to know them." These are considered some of the most dangerous places on the Internet. Strangers go into these forums meant for children and pose as a child just to "talk dirty" or sometimes take it a step further and meet an adolescent, privately.

Blogging (web logging) is another Internet activity that adolescents engage in to express themselves — with anonymity. Adolescents tend to post journals that elicit personal information and reveal their identity over time. It is important for them to learn how to maintain personal boundaries and keep their own and other people's personal information such as name, address, phone number, and secrets that they may have of others private. Kids must realize that anything posted on the Internet can be seen by anyone, whether it is a teacher or a college admissions officer who can do a background check on a child.

Go to www.netsmartz.org for more information on the Internet safety-education resource that has greatly helped children aged 5-17, parents, educators, law enforcement, and other community leaders gain awareness about these dangers on the Internet. They provide online and offline activities, games, Internet safety pledges, news articles, and activity cards designed to supplement the NetSmartz online activities. They also have created interactive presentations for elementary, middle, and high school students and communities (NetSmartz, 2009).

The glamorization of violent acts among everyday people, famous people, political leaders, and anti-government messages during times of political conflict can be viewed with regularity and very limited regulation has been instituted at this point. Though recently, Thailand has worked to block many pornographic or violent websites deemed dangerous by the government. The government has invited the public to submit sites to be blocked to help protect Thai youth from bad influences. Each month, hundreds of sites are submitted and then viewed by the Royal Thai Police website for consideration. This is a major initiative to reduce negative message exposure to Thai youth (Website ban, 2009).

According to extensive psychological research, violence can have profound effects on youth including (National Institute of Mental Health, 1982):

- Children may become less sensitive to the pain and suffering of others.
- Children may be more fearful of the world around them.
- Children may be more likely to behave in aggressive ways toward others.

Also:

- Children may be less likely to succeed academically (Children and television violence, 2005).

What can parents do to best regulate the influence of mass media on their child?

- Position a computer/television in a centrally located area of the residence, where it is used as a family resource/entertainment source.

- Purchase parental control software to protect children from inappropriate content on the Internet. There are also free website blocking downloads that are available that remove undesired websites from a child's view and prevent a child from spending a long time in chat rooms.

- Watch television with your child and discuss the happenings of a show and teach her/him to be critical of the messages given.

- Limit television viewing and/or computer use (when not needed for academic purposes) preferably to 1-hour a day during a school week and instill a reading rewards program for your child.

- Encourage your child to participate in extracurricular activities after school.

Questions to consider relating to violence and the mass media

➢ Can we trust what the government attempts to censor as truly being violent?

➢ What reinforcement is provided at movie theatres to ensure that children view age-appropriate movies and do not sneak in to see other movies?

➢ Why should children be allowed to watch violence when they are not allowed to watch non-violent "adult movies?"

➢ Why don't we look for a long-term solution that involves educating youth and adult populations, rather than developing different brands of "bandages" for all of these issues?

➢ What strategies can parents use to regulate new media activities on the Internet, video games, downloaded songs/videos, etc.?

➢ How do we protect children from dangers in the media when both parents work and children have more unsupervised time and opportunities for encounters with mass media?

➢ How do we get the media "on our side," rather than them rebutting with statements of "This is reality and if you don't like it, change the channel," or "Millions of people watch violence every day and they don't become criminals?"

The Effects of Imprisonment

Statistics on perpetrators and victims of crimes show that the two age groups that comprise the most encounters with violence are 18-24 year olds and 12-17 year olds, first and second, respectively. There are many forms of violence such as assault, robberies, rapes, and the ultimate display is murder. Homicide is the second leading cause of death among people aged 15-34. Gang violence takes on a heightened form of violence where drugs become linked to problems. Gang violence had increased substantially throughout the 1970s & 80s in the United States spreading throughout all 50 states where ages ranged from 12-21 years old. Nowadays, children as young as 8-years-old join gangs and continue being members well into their 30s and sometimes beyond (The Youth Violence Epidemic, 2009).

The United States imprisons more people than any other nation in the world. The U.S. incarcerates people for more diverse offenses and for a longer time frame than any other country. The U.S. imprisons more people for drug law violations than all of Western Europe. The United States houses 5% of the world's population and almost 25% of the world's prisoners (Liptak, 2008). Does this mean that the U.S. has the most violent society in the world out of all of the countries?

Experts have commented on what these prison figures purport as a reflection on our society in terms of how we handle education, poverty, urban development, health care, and child care. Each day more and more people are sent to prison, yet more and more crimes are being committed (Liptak, 2008). Why are so many people in prison? Is this a good thing that we have more people being locked up than being released?

Studies have been conducted determining which programs are most effective in preventing reoccurring violence among prisoners once they are released and return to the community. The most effective, designed program provided prisoners free higher education that allowed them to acquire a college degree. Studies performed in Massachusetts, California, and Indiana display startling breakthrough evidence that give scientists insight to the most effective means of reducing violence in society. Hundreds of inmates serving for the most serious crimes including murder, rape, and armed robbery obtained a college degree while in prison and less than 1% of those individuals returned to prison 30 years following prison release. Educating inmates has been proven to greatly benefit those leaving prison upon re-entering the community (Gilligan, 2001).

Certainly there has to be a price paid for committing a crime that fails to be in accordance with our local, state, and federal laws. The topic about what punishment fits a crime is debatable, but more importantly, what goals, if any, do we have in mind for those who have committed heinous crimes? The goal that is reached should coincide with the goal that we have for society and that is — to become EDUCATED.

"It isn't enough to talk about peace. One must believe in it. And it isn't enough to believe in it. One must work at it."

**-ELEANOR ROOSEVELT
(former First Lady of the U.S.)**

14.   DEPRESSION & SUICIDE

*A spring 2006 survey of nearly 95,000 students on 117 college/ university campuses in the U.S. indicates:

- "Nearly half of the students felt so depressed that it was difficult to function at least once during the academic year."

- "Sixteen percent felt that way on at least five occasions."

- "Nine percent thought about attempting suicide; one percent actually attempted."

- "Nearly two-thirds of students felt their situation to be hopeless at least once by all they had to do."

- "More than 93% had felt overwhelmed at least once by all that they had to do."

*Source: Walsh (2007) as cited in the *Pittsburgh Post-Gazette.*

The term "depression" arose later in the 19th century.   For 2000 years before, it was described as "melancholy."   Abraham Lincoln suffered from this "melancholy" for much of his adult life, but it was said to "fuel his greatness" (Shenk, 2005). Unfortunately, these feelings do not have similar effects for approximately 30,000 Americans that suffer from depression to the point of taking their own lives every year (TePastte, 2008).

Modern medicine does not give enough attention to social factors that contribute to depression. Depression can be caused by many factors including outside influences from our surroundings and a decrease in the functional balance of the primary neurotransmitters in the brain. Prescribing medicine for "treating the illness" is the route, most often, taken by medical experts. This is a big reason why the main factors of illness continue to go unnoticed or unrecognized.

The biomedical health model states that illness is a failure that appears in the human body that deviates from its normal state of balance. The body is ill and all attention is directed to illness treatment.

There is no orientation to the individual's well- being. This model indicates that the soul and body are to be treated separately. Therefore, all attention is directed on the treating of the biological imbalance and the accompanying symptoms, as opposed to analyzing social factors that are specifically impacting the individual (Giddens, 2001).

Medical specialists are regarded as experts that can treat illness where the focus is on the biological process that goes on within the body. This is a primary explanation for why this illness is treated with anti-depressants, psychotherapy, light therapy, physical exercises, and other methods. The responsibility for maintaining health or becoming ill is thus placed on the individual. The disease is instead free of cultural content. There are alternative practitioners that take into account body and soul as connected, taking into consideration the strong impact that social factors have on our bodies.

According to ancient Japanese physician, Kan Funajana (Tombak, 2005):

"A human being is an entity whose soul and body form a union. This is why it is not possible to heal the body without considering the state of the soul and vice versa."

Social factors impacting depression and suicide (Benokraitis, 2008):

> ➤ Women are more vulnerable than men and have more expectations and duties in today's society. Expectations include being a good worker, homemaker, parent, and being beautiful. They experience more physical, mental, and psychological abuse than men. Patriarchy continues to exist, to a large degree, in society where men hold the positions of power and authority.

> ➤ Problems within the family including the loss of a loved one, pregnancy, divorce, abuse, unemployment, etc.

> ➤ Childhood experiences of abuse.

> ➤ Social isolation due to intolerance of one's race, ethnicity, and/

or socioeconomic status. Long periods of loneliness can lead to a long lasting feeling of depression.

➢ Poverty. Children who grow up in impoverished environments are more vulnerable to abuse.

➢ Media's display of the "ideal image" resulting in many youth's obsession to be perfect.

➢ The rapid development of technology.

➢ Academic pressures to achieve at high levels.

➢ Not feeling understood by family, friends, teachers, and other close individuals.

➢ Too many happenings and responsibilities occurring in one's life.

According to the National Institute of Mental Health (2008), symptoms of depression may include the following:

- Persistent sadness, anxiety, or empty moods.
- Feelings of guilt, helplessness, worthlessness, hopelessness.
- Loss of interest in once pleasurable leisure activities.
- Loss of memory, concentration on tasks, and decision-making.
- Increased tiredness, loss of energy.
- Changes in appetite and weight.
- Poor self-image or self-esteem.
- Restlessness, irritability.
- Physical problems such as headaches, pain, and digestive complaints.
- Sleep disturbances.
- Suicidal thoughts or attempts.

These findings suggest that increasing numbers of depressive episodes from ages 16 to 21 were associated with poorer mental health, educational, and socioeconomic outcomes at ages 21–25 years (Fergusson et al., 2007).

Suicide: One of the most tragic consequences of depression

A very sad, but real, form of violence is suicide. The rate of suicide for 15-24 year olds has more than tripled since 1960 — making it the third leading cause of death among 15-24 year olds and the second leading cause of death among college-age youth. Although depression is more often diagnosed in women than men, men complete suicide more than women (CDC, 2005). White men complete over 72% of all suicides and 79% of them are accomplished with the use of firearms (Suicide and Depression, 2004).

I have the unfortunate experience as a public school teacher to have taught students who have taken their lives prematurely. It is, often times, overlooked or difficult to detect the warning signs of suicidal behavior, but the most important factor to realize is the root of the problem. A predominant view of suicide is that it is a "mental health" concern involving psychological factors of suffering, the inability to escape fear, and/or mental disorders/pressures (Suicide, 2009).

The inevitable cause of suicide is the implication of some form of shame and guilt felt and their powerful effects to cause extreme feelings of pain and how it motivates emotions of violence. In contrast, but in relation to shame, is the feeling of guilt. Shame motivates anger and violence toward others, while guilt motivates these feelings within oneself (Gilligan, 2003).

People that feel shame perceive the shame as stemming from other people and target the anger toward those individuals, while people who experience guilt perceive the problem as being within themselves and some of these people believe that the only way to eliminate the guilt is to eliminate its source — oneself (Gilligan, 2003).

Keeping firearms out of the household and prescription drugs in a safe, inconspicuous location helps reduce impulses to commit suicide. The best advice that I have given parents, family members, teachers, coaches, and other adults active in a child's life over the years to help intervene is to discuss feelings of shame and guilt with children and greatly emphasize open and honest lines of communication. From this point, we can better examine many of the warning signs for suicidal behavior and gain awareness for a child's various reactions to distress.

The good news about depression is that most people with it can and do recover (Henderson et al., 2004). Safe and effective methods of prevention and treatment for depression are widely available. Various forms of psychotherapy have been successful in treating depression including talking, behavior, cognitive/behavioral, and interpersonal therapies (TePastte, 2008).

*Warning Signs of Suicidal Behavior

- Poor communication with parents.
- Increased risk-taking behaviors.
- Drastic changes (personality, eating, sleeping, studying, clothing, friends, likes/dislikes, appearance, etc.).
- Social isolation.
- Morbid thoughts.
- Violent or rebellious outbursts.
- Giving away personal possessions.
- Apathy.
- Increased sensitivity.
- Actual talk of suicide.
- Recent suicide of a friend or family member.
- Saying that they have nothing to live for.
- Attempted suicides before.
- Experimenting with alcohol, prescription drugs, and/or illicit drugs.
- Impulsive, prone to accidents.
- Rejection by a boyfriend or girlfriend.

*Source: Preventing Adolescent Suicide (1996).

Strategies to help a child who appears depressed or suicidal

- Provide emotional support, be patient, and listen to the individual. Encourage open conversation realizing that your assistance may be the difference between life and death. If a

child is unwilling to communicate with you, encourage her/
him to speak with someone trustworthy.

- Invite the individual to participate in an activity (e.g. exercise, watch a movie, play a game, attend a social gathering, etc.) to keep her/his mind diverted on other events. If the person declines, refrain from pushing too much. Many demands may increase feelings of failure.

- Provide an atmosphere that is positive and free of negative thinking.

- Remind a child that life is full of ups and downs and that a feeling of sadness will pass in time. Relate to a child an experience in your life that made you feel really down for a while, how you thought it would never get better, and how the situation actually got better.

- Offer hope to the individual by helping her/him set goals and priorities. Dividing large tasks into smaller pieces help relieve anxiety and pressure to accomplish an entire task.

- Never ignore comments about suicide and if you have attempted other strategies that were unsuccessful, report the individual to a specialized expert in the areas of depression and suicide.

Suicide occurs, most often, among individuals aged 85 and over suffering from chronic illnesses (Suicide and Depression, 2004). However, suicide has been and still remains a problem targeting youth. Several recent studies have found a link between negative body image, depression, and suicide. Suicidal thoughts and attempts are much more common when young people perceive themselves as too fat, regardless of how much they weigh. In the next section, it is discussed how striving to achieve an image, often seen in advertisements, can become an individual's greatest obsession.

15. ANABOLIC STEROIDS

Bigger is not better

We hear about select athletes who test positive for steroid use in track & field, cycling, football, basketball, baseball, and hockey (among many sports) and walk away with fines imparted or medals taken away. What you do not hear in the news, very often, is the story of a young athlete who started with a dream to become a college or professional athlete that resulted in a radical change of personality where depression and aggression plagued her/his life and the repeated suicide attempts that ensued. The dream shifts to one of survival where family and close friends must step in to take action and get an individual much needed help.

There are no controlled scientific studies of "roid rage" but many researchers in the field indicate the use of anabolic androgenic steroids (AAS) as a likely contributing factor in the violent tragedy involving former WWE wrestler Chris Benoit in the killings of his wife and son followed by his suicide. Benoit's doctor, Dr. Phil Astin, prescribed a ten-month supply of anabolic steroids to Chris Benoit every three to four weeks between May 2006 and May 2007. Former professional wrestlers who used steroids in their career indicate that athletes use these to gain strength and size and not all of the time does one become hostile, but there are "moments of uncontrollable rage" (Dornin and Reiss, 2007).

Former wrestler, Del Wilkes states:

"You can feel it coming on but there's nothing you can do about it. The next thing you know, a minor argument has gone into a full-fledged rage, when you've got your hands around somebody's neck. You're in a fight and doing things you wouldn't normally do. The drugs can also cause 'tremendous' depression when guys are coming off steroids after they've been on it for a long period of time" (Dornin and Reiss, 2007).

Anabolic steroids are performance-enhancing drugs that are synthetically produced and are closely related to the male sex hormone testosterone. A growing number of teenage boys and girls use potentially unhealthy products ranging from growth hormone to injectable steroids at least weekly to improve appearance or strength (Steroid Abuse By School Age Children, 2007).

A recent study has been conducted from the University of Michigan's Institute for Social Research stating that the percent of twelfth graders who have taken steroids has more than tripled in the last ten years and is slowly coming back down, but ever so slowly. Still, over 300,000 students between the eighth and twelfth grade have been shown to use anabolic steroids in the U.S. (NIDA, 2008).

Why do so many kids resort to steroids to get stronger?

Steroids work! That is why. Popping pills and using gels and injectable solutions are easy and render quick, efficient results. I exercised at a local fitness club for years and saw transformations of people's bodies in a very short period. I would speak to various steroid users and ask them why they continued to "shoot up" despite knowing all of the potential side effects. Their responses included, "I can get to that next level that much easier," "People admire me for how I look." You will hear about athletes taking steroids or see body builders displaying these superhuman bodies if you watch or listen to the media. This seems to intrigue, more than turn away, today's youth from experimenting with such a potentially lethal weapon.

Coaches have a very influential role in this matter. They have to be careful what messages they give to their athletes. "Put on 20 pounds if you want to start for my team," "Be like Bobby and add on ten more pounds of muscle if you want a chance to play." These messages plant a seed of desperation for many athletes that become rooted. They figure that in order to have a chance to become a star athlete, they have to resort to drastic measures to make it happen. Coaches of all sports have to be careful when talking to their players — whether it is football, baseball, basketball, hockey, wrestling, swimming, or golf.

Teenagers and young men see the chiseled look of the models pictured on billboards, in catalogs, and on television and desire to be that way. This emergence of steroid use has led researchers to believe that these individuals are suffering from muscle dysmorphia, which is also referred to as "reverse anorexia" or "manorexia." The individual has an irrational obsession with perceived flaws in appearance. Much like anorexia nervosa, steroid abuse continues despite the individual experiencing harmful effects because she/he never feels big enough. It has been referred to as "the secret crisis of male body obsession" — not limited to males, but mainly (Pope et al., 2000). Dreams of having an ideal, intimidating physique can render the most intimidating and harsh blow to a young abuser's body and future. Many are aware of the dangers, but many more do not care.

Do the risks outweigh the reward?

Reward

> Stronger looking body with increased leanness, muscle mass, strength, and definition.

What are some of the potential physical and psychological side effects?

> Severe acne.
> Hair loss.
> Growth stunt (growth plates close prematurely in a young person).
> Fatty deposits under the nipples (breast development).
> High blood pressure and heart disease.
> Strokes and blood clots.
> Headaches.
> Joint pain.
> Sterility/impotence.
> Shrinkage/loss of function of testicles.
> Increase risk of tendon injuries.
> Mood swings.
> Depression.
> Aggression.
> Paranoia.
> Nervousness.
> Extreme irritability.
> Delusions.
> Impaired judgments (feeling invincible).
> DEATH!

*Females can specifically suffer from:

✓ Abnormalities in one's menstrual cycle.

✓ Acquiring male characteristics including an increase in facial hair, deepening of the voice, reduction in breast size, and an increase in clitoris size.

*Source: Steroid Abuse By School Age Children (2007). Note: Little research has been conducted on the long-term effects of steroid abuse.

There are many different types of common steroids, drugs used to treat negative effects of anabolic steroids, steroid alternatives, and masking agents for steroids that are currently used.

*Common examples of oral and injectable steroids

Oral Steroids	Injectable Steroids
• Anadrol® (oxymetholone) • Oxandrin® (oxandrolone) • Dianabol® (methandrostenolone) • Winstrol® (stanozolol)	• Deca-Durabolin® (nandrolone decanoate) • Durabolin® (nandrolone phenpropionate) • Depo-Testosterone® (testosterone cypionate) • Equipoise® (boldenone undecylenate) (veterinary product)®

*Source: Steroid Abuse By School Age Children (2007).
Visit the NIDA's steroids-specific website for further information on the effects of anabolic-androgenic steroids and information on healthy alternatives.

Physical attractiveness, strength, aggressiveness, confidence, and being in control have been deemed desirable qualities for men to have and should be seen as major factors for many individuals using steroids (Schwerin and Corcoran, 1992). The visual culture represented in all facets of mass media has a serious hook on today's youth. Magazines, advertisements, movies, and television shows are hot markets that boast today's cultural norms with the intent to sell products that people wish to see or have.

"The Adonis Complex" is seen in a growing number of males who seek to achieve physical perfection and become a specimen of desire. Researchers have postulated that this phenomenon has to do with the rising power of women in society. The male body becomes the last place for men trying to preserve their "masculinity." Their perception is that more women may be obtaining higher-ranking and paid jobs than past years, but they are not able to lift so much weight as men can (Pope et al., 2000).

Clearly, these societal expectations for being valued, manly, and desirable are clear, but what are the perceptions about those who take anabolic steroids. What do non-users think of male steroid users?

Analyses indicate two findings (Schwerin and Corcoran, 1992):

1. Subjects view a bodybuilding steroid-user significantly more negatively than a diet conscious bodybuilder or an athletically active individual.

2. Subjects view a cocaine-using bodybuilder and a steroid-using bodybuilder similarly.

Such steroid-enhanced individuals who are ubiquitous in the mass media display unrealistic models of masculinity. These bodies are greatly valued and as a result, mass media capitalizes on this desire. A vision of the "ideal-body image" for a male becomes distorted. Social constructs are created and exist as a school of thought for how valued males should appear. In the final analysis, steroid use takes away what one attempts to achieve — feeling valued.

"In a hundred years, it will not matter what my bank account was, the type of house I lived in, or in the kinds of clothes I wore, but the world may be much different because I was important in the life of a child."

-ANONYMOUS

16.   EATING DISORDERS

There exists a norm in today's society in which everyone wishes to stay young forever. As we age, we see evidence of youth disappearing and begin to look for magical formulas that will reverse aging and maintain youth. Sculpting the perfect body in all of its parts — through surgeries, reading diet and exercise books, overexercising, and obsessing on healthy food consumption, can lead to serious life-long problems.

A case study was conducted with a woman in her mid-20s and she indicated:

> *"Plastic surgery is a fine line between necessity and a horribly addictive downward spiral and I was noticing that every time I looked in the mirror, there was nothing I could do. I felt distorted, without exaggeration, as I always knew I had beauty, but it was happening; every surgery was notching away at that once confidence."*

Many individuals are obsessed with achieving the perfect body and going to the gym is no longer a choice, but has become a necessity in society's eyes (Compulsive Exercise, 2007). Most of the time, people think about their inside organs when they feel pain or even worse when a disease is diagnosed. According to Chris Shilling (2003), in postmodern society, the body becomes like a machine, perceived as a body without organs, which can be reconstructed and maintained by exercises, diets, and health programs.

Five percent of the population in the world (especially women) suffers from eating disorders, most commonly anorexia and bulimia. Usually anorexia starts first and finishes with bulimia because not many individuals can continue starving (Giordano, 2005).

Eating disorders run rampant among millions of boys and girls around the globe. Dr. Ruth Striegel-Moore, Ph.D. (2005), a professor of psychology at Wesleyan University in Connecticut, proclaims that an estimated seven million girls/women and one million boys/men struggle with eating disorders — such as anorexia nervosa, bulimia nervosa, and binge-eating disorder in the United States. This problem is not simply isolated to the Western hemisphere, but has become widespread cutting across gender, race, and ethnicity. Individuals, as young as preschool aged children, are aware of their body physiques and how it compares with other children their age.

Anorexia nervosa

Anorexia nervosa is a disorder characterized by "deliberate weight loss, induced and sustained by the patient." It is a specific mental illness where by an individual has a "dread of fatness and flabbiness of body contour." A person sets a low weight standard, severely restricts caloric intake, and becomes malnourished to a certain severity (Giordano, 2005: 24).

Anorexia has one of the highest death rates of any mental health condition. It hits all age groups but affects mainly, but not limited to, adolescents and young women (90-95%). It is important to understand that this is an illness and many individuals who become afflicted do not fit the typical anorexic profile (American Psychiatric Association, 2006).

Experts state that the earlier the disorder is spotted and treated, the greater the chances for full recovery. The consensus is that those patients who see a reason to get better and work with professionals to build strategies will get better (Berkman et al., 2007).

*Warning Signs of Anorexia

- Sudden decrease in weight.

- Dry and yellowish skin.

- Refusal to eat meals and/or specific foods.

- A dramatic decrease in clothes size.

- Frequent comments of feeling "fat" or overweight despite losing weight.

- Anxiety about gaining weight or being "fat."

- Denial of hunger.

- Development of food rituals (e.g. eating foods in certain orders, excessive chewing, rearranging food on a plate).

- Giving regular excuses to avoid mealtimes or situations pertaining to food.

- Excessive exercise despite fatigue, illness, injury, or weather.

- Withdrawal from usual friends and activities.

- Lack of a menstrual cycle (for females).

- Behaviors and attitudes indicating that weight loss, dieting, and control of food are becoming the main focus and concerns.

Potential Health Consequences of Anorexia

- Decrease in bone density — increasing the risk for osteoporosis.
- Muscle wasting and weakness.
- Severe dehydration — which can result in kidney failure.
- Fainting, lethargy, and overall weakness.
- Dry hair and skin. Hair loss is common.
- Growth of a downy layer of hair called lanugo all over the body, including the face — in an effort to keep the body warm.
- Abnormally slow heart rate and low blood pressure, which mean that the heart muscle is changing. The risk for heart failure rises as heart rate and blood pressure levels sink lower and lower.

*Source: NEDA, Anorexia Nervosa (2006).

Bulimia nervosa

Bulimia nervosa is a disorder characterized by "repeated bouts of overeating and an excessive preoccupation with the control of body weight." These actions lead to a "pattern of overeating followed by vomiting or use of purgatives" (Giordano, 2005: 24).

As with anorexia, more females than males (approximately 80%) suffer from bulimia. The binge-eating episodes mask deep-rooted unresolved psychological issues that have presented themselves as serious pressures in an individual's life (Gidwani and Rome, 1997).

These forces affect self-image and self-esteem. Both anorexia and bulimia have similar ramifications in causing feelings of depression and abuse (emotional, verbal, physical, and sexual) (Giordano, 2005). The result of anorexia and bulimia on one's health is similar, but how are they different in their unique course to disaster?

The ability to spot a bulimic is not that easy, as compared to many (but not all) suffering anorexics. With bulimia, they could appear to have a normal body weight or even be slightly overweight and unless you catch them in the act of bingeing or purging, you may never guess that they have a problem.

Bulimics have a different medical concern from anorexics in that a constant purging of food causes tooth decay and renders many digestive tract problems. The esophagus can be severely damaged due to the constant regurgitation of stomach acids. As a result, the body can become severely dehydrated, have an electrolyte imbalance (disturbing potassium levels in the body), have an irregular heartbeat, and have bowel problems. Bulimics can die from ulcers, ruptures in the intestinal lining, kidney failure, strokes, and heart attacks (NEDA, 2006).

*Warning Signs of Bulimia

- Evidence of binge-eating — including disappearance of large amounts of food in short time frames or the existence of wrappers and containers indicating the consumption of large amounts of food.

- Excessive exercise despite fatigue, illness, injury, or weather.

- Unusual swelling of the cheeks or jaw area.

- Calluses on the back of the hands and knuckles from self-induced vomiting.

- Discoloration or staining of the teeth.

- Creation of schedules or rituals to make time for binge-and-purge sessions.

- Withdrawal from regular friends and activities.

- In general, behaviors and attitudes indicating that weight loss, dieting, and control of food are becoming a main concern.

*Potential Health Consequences of Bulimia

- Electrolyte imbalances that can lead to irregular heartbeats and possibly heart failure and death. Electrolyte imbalance is caused by dehydration and loss of potassium and sodium from the body as a result of purging behaviors.

- Inflammation and possible rupture of the esophagus from frequent vomiting.

- Tooth decay and staining from stomach acids released during frequent vomiting.

- Chronic, irregular bowel movements and constipation as a result of laxative abuse.

- Gastric rupture is an uncommon but possible side effect of binge eating.

*Source: NEDA, Bulimia Nervosa (2006).

Binge eating disorder

A third eating disorder classified as eating beyond the point of satiety at least twice a week is known as "binge eating." This eating disorder is characterized by episodes of binge eating without the purging events that follow. This has become the biggest eating disorder in the United States, outnumbering those individuals suffering from anorexia and bulimia combined (Hudson et al., 2007).

This behavior of out-of-control eating is a contributor to a rise in obesity. With the heavy stresses and responsibilities that people have throughout the day, their life may feel out of control and food is, often times, used to solace feelings of anxiety and depression. People who indulge in such manner express shame and guilt over their eating behaviors (Binge Eating Disorder, 2003).

*Potential Health Consequences of Binge Eating

- High blood pressure,
- High cholesterol levels,
- Heart disease,
- Diabetes mellitus,
- Gallbladder disease.

*Source: Binge Eating Disorder (2003).

*Psychiatric researchers at Harvard University Medical School indicate that among the U.S. population:

- ➢ 1% of women and 0.3% of men suffer from anorexia.
- ➢ 1.5% of women and 0.5% of men suffer from bulimia.
- ➢ 3.5% of women and 2% of men suffer from binge eating disorder.

*Source: Fox News: Survey: Binging Most Common Eating Disorder in America: http://www.foxnews.com/story/0,2933,249481,00.html?sPage=fnc/health/mentalhealth.

Social factors causing eating disorders

Eating disorders are likely to result from many different social factors including social pressures, family influences, genetic predisposition, neurophysiological vulnerability, moral values, and personality variables such as perfectionism, need for control, and low self-esteem (Giordano, 2005). The major causes mentioned for developing such disorders include experiencing abuse or neglect and a pressure to restrict food intake due to peer or society pressure of how one should physically appear to be considered attractive. Dr. Striegel-Moore states that she has seen that these individuals who suffer from eating disorders all share the same psychological implication: a miscued self-perception (Striegel-Moore, 2005).

A negative body image can lead to a severe loss of self-esteem, resulting in depression — as well as eating disorders. The social, emotional, physical, financial, and moral damages that millions of people incur due to this endless pursuit of beauty cannot be accurately measured. Research suggests that nearly 8 out of 10 girls and young women feel dissatisfied with their body appearance and desire to lose weight. Females especially are concerned about their body weight and shape. Males are more concerned about the size and strength of their body, building muscles, and sculpting a chiseled appearance, if they wish to fit in as a "real man" (Fox, 1997).

Individuals with eating disorders have a wish to be good looking and they focus a great deal on their body image. Various taunting, criticism of one's appearance, and a negative personal evaluation of one's body take place where girls who suffer from eating disorders associate a burly body with abnormality, otherness, shame, feeling outcast from society, and stigmatized. In contrast, to be slender means to be beautiful, good, valued, happy, and to live a productive life (Belekeviciute, 2007).

Mass media with its popular, slim, sexual, beautiful woman's body appearance can also be a major reason why girls "catch the illness" (Belekeviciute, 2007). According to Ann Marie Palm (1996), models became taller, younger, and thinner during the 1960s. Society watches them and tries to match those ideals that propagate such unhealthy body forms, the slenderness mania — which contribute to the onset of eating disorders.

Today, the media bombards youth with images of thin girls from all ethnicities and that they should be working out and dieting to sculpt the perfect body. There are cultural messages being given that are different. For instance, it has often been more sexually appealing for an African-American woman to carry more weight than a Caucasian woman (Altabe, 1998).

Anorexia and bulimia are very complex disorders that root in some unresolved emotional conflicts or expressions. A series of traumatic events from early on largely contribute to these behaviors, whether it is major occurrences like severe physical or mental abuse or less severe traumas where expectations for being thin strongly prevail from family, past relationships, or society — in general (Benokraitis, 2008).

Family dynamics factor greatly in a child's perception on what is deemed appropriate and acceptable. The family that focuses on externals such as appearance and/or achievements as important and how others will perceive them has a strong influence on giving power to the importance of self-image. Having an overprotective family can squash one's formation of identity and individuality and leave one wondering, "Who am I?" The chaotic family lacks rules and consistency and children from these families can, often times, experience physical and/or mental abuse on a consistent basis.

Most girls with eating disorders come from problematic families that experience problems such as violence, divorce, alcoholism, loss of a close person, criticism of appearance, and a distant relationship between parents and children. The importance of friends' opinions (that are influenced by ideals of society) can also affect an individual to be conscious about one's body. (Belekeviciute, 2007).

Many people who suffer from eating disorders realize that they do have a problem, but cannot find a solution. A path to achieve slenderness may originate from diets and the propagation of a healthy lifestyle that later can cause eating disorders (Belekeviciute, 2007).

Anorexic and bulimic girls encounter many health problems and usually experience only negative feelings caused by outside factors. These, in turn, strongly influence social relationships and greatly alter everyday life. Girls also lose volition to interact with other human beings, devalue their own bodies and personalities, and ultimately become more passive (Belekeviciute, 2007).

*Below is a body image test that parents can give to see where their child's level of self-confidence is in regards to their personal appearance.

1. Does consuming a small amount of food make you feel fat?
2. Do you worry or obsess about your body not being small, thin, or good enough?
3. Are you concerned your body is not muscular or strong enough?
4. Do you avoid wearing certain clothes because they make you feel fat?
5. Do you feel badly about yourself because you don't like your body?
6. Have you ever disliked your body?
7. Do you want to change something about your body?
8. Do you compare yourself to others and feel that you fail in comparison?
9. Have you avoided sports or working out because you didn't want to be seen in gym clothes?

*Source: Adapted from *Body Image* by Cindy Maynard, MS, RD Health and Medical Writer/Registered Dietitian (2007).

If a child answers "YES" to 3 or more questions, then she/he may have a negative body image.

How can we prevent today's youth from acquiring an eating disorder?

- Evaluate your own attitudes, beliefs, and behaviors about food, weight, body image, physical appearance, health, and exercise.

- Educate children on healthy eating habits of eating when they are hungry, rather than inadvertently telling them not to eat something that could make them fat and depriving them of a meal. Encourage balanced eating of a variety of foods.

- Love, respect, listen to, acknowledge, encourage, appreciate, and value children out loud.

- Help develop a child's self-esteem, self-worth, and self-identity early on. Feeling confident and having a sense of balance and control in life are key factors for a nurturing foundation. Develop a value system based on internal values that focus on cooperation, individuality, caring for others, self-awareness, ambition, motivation, curiosity, confidence, and a good sense of humor.

- Allow for a child to freely discuss her/his concerns. Body image disorders arise from a variety of bottled up physical, emotional, social, and family problems. The more open the lines of communication, the less suppressed the emotions, thus helping to prevent the manifestation of an eating disorder.

- Directly address the cultural obsession of slenderness (females) and strength (males) as a physical, psychological, and moral issue. Have young people think critically about the intentions of the mass media in their portrayal of an ideal image.

- Foster a child's self-respect and respect for others in a wide array of environments by promoting diversity in race, gender, weight, athleticism, intelligence, and popularity. Promote the importance of one's character, rather than physical appearance.

- Involve a child in various group activities that allow her/him to get physical activity in something safe and enjoyable. Help children accept and feel good about their bodies. Every "BODY" should be free!

- If you suspect that your child may have an eating disorder, you may want to seek advice from a professional to see what further steps need to be taken in order to accurately address the problem.

Competitive events, beauty pageants, schools, and the workplace often set the stage for winners and losers, getting the prize or not being good enough, landing the job or not having "what it takes," being popular, good-looking, and cool, or being unattractive, out of shape and/or a geek/outcast. The story of a little girl who enjoyed life participating in sports, music, and doing well at school academically and with her peers and then suddenly fighting an illness that induces her to starve herself to the point of near death is becoming all too commonplace for girls and a growing number of boys at a younger and younger age. To eat or not to eat — there is no question!

17.   LAZY LIFESTYLE

After over four decades of government health campaigns promoting health and education in the classroom about eating well and exercising, we have strived to make moderate progress for a while and now have suddenly made a drastic 360-degree turn to where we began. We have a problem on our hands where almost anything that we desire is a click away — clothes, food, books, music, even making friends, or going out on a date. The most important factor that has escaped the information super highway is and may very well always be — HEALTH!

It's a person's choice: To be (healthy) or not to be?

The message is clear. More than ever before in history, children need to get up and MOVE MORE...NOW! We often hear from a child, "I'm bored. What can I do?" The decision "to do" and not "to sit" should be the undisputed answer. Children have an innate tendency to have a high energy level and it is important to direct a child's energy into something meaningful and productive. Building a strong body at a young age and continuing to do so throughout life is fundamental to long-term health.

A lazy lifestyle can lead to some serious health concerns for a young person's future. For instance, diabetes is part of a metabolic syndrome where an individual is not able to produce a sufficient supply of a hormone called insulin to regulate blood sugar levels. Many children as young as 6-years-old develop adult-onset diseases — such as type 2 (adult) diabetes, hypertension, bone stress, etc (Kiess et al., 2003).

Parents are part of a very stressed out working population who, often times, lack the sufficient energy to do all that much when they come home. With many parents living a busy, on the go, stressed out lifestyle, they pick up more fast food meals for their family. This repeated pattern has many negative implications for overall health and wellness, which will be discussed in the next section pertaining to obesity.

How often children play video games, talk on the phone, watch television, and spend time on the computer (that isn't school related), translates into how often they do not get a healthy dose of physical activity in their daily schedule. These multimedia pieces of equipment often take the place of a parent. They act as the babysitter for a few hours until it is time to eat and then time to go to bed. It is important to set guidelines for a child to be able to use a multimedia activity for one hour (or to a parent's discretion) after a minimum of one hour of some form of physical activity has been performed.

I can foresee that one day most, if not all, places of employment will require physical activity to be a part of every employee's working day. Physical activity is a central part of a healthy lifestyle and I feel that the time will come when all employers get smart and make it mandatory that people of all ages, shapes, and sizes obtain daily activity at their jobs. This will save companies millions of dollars in health care costs where insurance companies will offer lower rates with a wellness program offered to employees.

Critics may feel that this could be considered discrimination against severely overweight or obese individuals? I would like to view this instead as a free wake up call for the out of shape or lazy worker to get healthy and moving more. It is obvious that society is headed down a dark, unhealthy road looming with severe health problems, if changes are not instituted soon. There is not much we can do about having fast foods, video games, television, and computers in the world — but there is something that we can do in regards to choices we make about being or not being physically active.

Factors that contribute to a child's physical activity and nutrition at school:

- The availability of safe playgrounds.
- Requirements for physical education.
- School nutrition policies.
- Types of foods sold at school fundraisers.
- Foods served at classroom parties.
- Information and education given to parents and adults about choosing better snacks at home.
- Participation in youth sports.
- Number of fast-food restaurants in the area.

State testing requirements help to keep students alerted to their health and fitness level (to a certain degree). Students in grades four, six, eight, and ten are required to take the Physical Fitness Assessment in many states, which usually measures the following parameters: upper-body strength, abdominal strength, flexibility, and running ability. Standards vary depending on age group and state. For instance, 8-year old girls must be able to touch their toes with legs straight, do 6 push-ups in 18 seconds, do 18 abdominal curls or crunches, and run a mile in 11 minutes and 15 seconds. A 15-year old boy must accomplish touching his toes and reaching beyond with legs straight, do 16 push-ups in 48 seconds, do 16 abdominal curls, and run a mile in 7 minutes and 30 seconds (Mauriello, 2005).

The state average in Connecticut for students passing all four parts of the test in 2005 was 35%. This ranked Connecticut at the top for the fittest children in the country. Connecticut requires 30 minutes of physical education a week for children in kindergarten through second-grade, 45 minutes weekly for third through fifth grade and 90 minutes weekly for middle school students. High school students must receive one credit to graduate, which is equivalent to daily exercise of one year of high school out of four years (Mauriello, 2005). These statistics should drive home a major point that we are in the midst of a crisis across our nation, but it is certainly within our grasp to prevent it. It is important to come together as a society and gain the knowledge necessary to effectively address it.

What specific efforts are being made in the schools to get kids moving more?

Whatever the approach to reform, teachers and support professionals are stepping up with creative approaches to incorporate increased nutritional education and physical activity into the schools. Brockway Elementary School in Pennsylvania has a day called "Walking Wednesdays" where about 100-200 students along with 10-30 adults walk to school. To fund this program, the school applied for and received a ten thousand dollar grant from the Blue Cross Blue Shield along with several mini-grants. At Brockway, one teacher at every grade level is trained in a nutritional curriculum. Also, this school has a Fun and Fitness after-school program with noncompetitive games and activities and cooking demonstrations to educate children about what is healthy and what is not healthy (Crute, 2005).

Carol Goodrow, a special education resource room teacher, created a running, writing, and nutrition program called "Happy Feet, Healthy Food" for the students at Birch Grove Primary in Tolland, Connecticut. A very active approach to increasing physical activity levels of children is taken each Friday morning and after school on Mondays and Thursdays during the school year. The students partake in a run with Goodrow and following that, they settle down and record their thoughts in their running journals. Goodrow has her classroom decorated with pictures of her runners enjoying healthy snacks and words of healthy foods on the ceiling. She reinforces good nutrition when children bring in healthy foods. Goodrow states, "I don't force anything. We talk about nutrition informally and I praise kids for bringing in healthy foods" (Crute, 2005).

In Kalispell, Montana, an outstanding effort has been made by a physical education teacher, Ross Darner, at Evergreen High School to implement summer fitness for children. He noticed that many children were sedentary and in the house quite a bit while their parents were at work. Many of these parents were unable to send their children to expensive trips or camps. With the help of Action for Healthy Kids, Darner raised enough funds to create a state-of-the-art fitness room that has a climbing wall, fitness and weight machines, heart monitors, and a great summer staff. He gained funds by obtaining a Physical Education Program (PEP) grant for nearly ninety thousand dollars, having a fund-raising carnival, and acquiring the support from local businesses (Crute, 2005).

Darner has modern equipment to measure children's blood pressure, body fat, strength, and flexibility. In the program's first year in 2003, about one-half of the fifth and sixth graders and some seventh and eighth graders, including obese children, volunteered to partake in weightlifting and cardiovascular workouts. Darner noticed that children who completed the program benefited and that their blood pressure dropped to healthy states (Crute, 2005).

The above examples provided are a limited number of schools across the U.S. that is waging the war against physical inactivity. To compensate for sedentary activities throughout the course of a school day, teachers are beginning to make efforts to incorporate physical activity into an already jam-packed curriculum and to include an academic piece into gym classes. Educators across the nation have shared the efforts that they have made to fight inactivity in the classroom. For instance, some math teachers have students playing different games while they are running. I also like the idea of team games where a student has to get an answer correct and then run to tag her/his teammate. This promotes an active, cooperative environment.

In my science classes, we would have inquiry-based laboratory experiments studying the effect of physical activity on one's heart rate, how different muscles fatigue, take nature walks to study the flora and fauna of ecology, design skits to act out various concepts, etc. At the very beginning of class on Friday mornings, the students are allowed to perform their favorite "dance of joy" standing near their seats with the intent to get their blood flowing and become energized for class.

What can parents do to get their kids moving more?

- Get a child involved in an age-appropriate activity that involves physical exertion from an early age. Expose a child to many different forms of aerobic exercise and allow them to choose what they would like to play (within safe and acceptable guidelines).

- Be a role model for good health. Participate in physical activity with your child and keep it fun so that your child wants to continue the activity.

- Encourage activity over exercise. Keeping it fun and allowing a child to choose the special activity is more exciting than "having to exercise."

- Limit the amount of time that your child spends doing a sedentary activity. School-aged children should not be inactive for periods lasting more than 2 hours; younger children should not have an inactivity period for more than 1 hour (Your Child & A Healthy Lifestyle, 2009).

- Establish a regular schedule for when your child is able to participate in physical activities.

- Assign your child a chore that involves some physical activity each day.

*Here are the current activity recommendations for children, taken from the National Association for Sport and Physical Education (NASPE):

Age	Minimum Daily Activity	Comments
Infant	No specific requirements	Physical activity should encourage motor development
Toddler	1 1/2 hours	30 minutes planned physical activity **AND** 60 minutes unstructured physical activity (free play)
Preschooler	2 hours	60 minutes planned physical activity **AND** 60 minutes unstructured physical activity (free play)
School age	1 hour or more	Break up into bouts of 15 minutes or more

*Source: Your Child & A Healthy Lifestyle (2009): http://www.tricycletour. co.za/advice.aspx.

A growing number of schools are jumping on the bandwagon and implementing school-wide programs within the core curricula, physical education classes, and peer groups with the effort to prevent obesity through improving diets and activity habits of children. A broad range of factors affects children's actual energy intake/expenditure throughout a school day such as a well-devised health program that promotes and teaches a healthy diet and physical activity, school policies that determine the amount of physical activity required throughout a school week, available healthy foods at lunch that are fresh and attractive, and the safety of the surrounding community for children to walk/bicycle home from school and/or play in the neighborhoods (Dietz, 2001).

School-based physical education requirements have statistically shown a drop off.   From 1991-2003, the percent of high school students that enrolled in daily physical education classes has dropped from 42% to 28%. In 2005, legislatures in 44 states introduced bills to increase or reform school physical education.   However, a new study suggests that mandating more time in gym classes may not result in more exercise or weight loss among American children due to contributing factors such as the amount of engaged vigorous exercise, the type of strength-building activity, and the duration of the exercise (Cawley et al., 2006).

Schools should require daily physical activity and a comprehensive health curriculum.   These two classes should have assessments as a mandatory part of the curriculum just as students are held responsible in their core academic subjects.   Administrators should regularly evaluate physical activity instruction, programs, and facilities. Schools should also set aside money for equipment and supervision for after school activities. Establishing policies that promote lifelong physical activity is necessary for a child's overall well-being in the long run.

18. OBESITY

Welcome to a world where health and fitness are still the craze and will continue to be for a very long time, yet seemingly not the norm. Who is to blame for such a far-reaching shift in pattern? The most common of behaviors that we long for out of children and adults, which is not as prevalent as before, is physical activity. Today's society has been altered from the days when kids played stickball and rode bicycles with their friends for hours to now where young people have video game marathons and read the next great children's novel for hours on end.

These have become acceptable leisure activities for today's youth. The problem isn't necessarily in the activities, but rather in the excessive time frame spent on them. Who is responsible for such a transformation of youth — compared to generations of the past? Better yet, what actions are being implemented to reverse this curse of low activity and rising body mass indices? Are they proving to be successful?

Various topics related to childhood obesity discussed include:

- Physical inactivity in today's youth (television, computers, video games' effect on this generation of children in relation to the development of overweight/obesity).

- Parenting education on early feeding behaviors and implications for food preferences later in life.

- Society's role and responsibility (restaurants, schools, legislature, etc.) in fighting this growing epidemic for today's youth and their future.

- Adult social and psychological outcomes of childhood obesity.

Children's overall mental and physical wellness has become one of the hot topics of the 21st century with concerns of today's youth facing graver challenges ahead. Experts are predicting that two-thirds of young people will become obese by the time they reach 50-years-old (Dietz, 2004). Communities around the country are beginning to put forth children's needs at school to prevent this from happening. They realize that these needs in many ways match the needs of adults at the work place: healthy nutrition + physical activity during the day = better overall behavior and academic performance during the day. Grants are being written, as we speak, to acquire federal funding for health and wellness programs for today's youth — in the form of health education or actual health and fitness programs at schools.

Childhood obesity has grown to epidemic levels across a large population of the world. Globally, over 22 million children under the age of five are overweight, as are 155 million school-age children (IFIC, 2006). North America, Europe, and parts of the Western Pacific have the highest prevalence of overweight children — approximately 20 to 30%. Research conducted in this study targeted the implications of childhood obesity for long-term potential consequences physically, socially, and emotionally. The focus is on early intervention measures that have been and can be taken to prevent any harmful, life-long effects (James, 2006). How schools, families, and communities collaborate to take a stand on this issue is vital to their success in developing specific strategies to formulate potential answers for solving this problem.

A focus lies in the psychological nature of obese children and how to develop strategies effective to improve self-esteem during these transitory years of childhood and how to improve daily activity functions in order to have higher energy levels and motivation in and out of a school environment. How to thwart the future dependence that people would have on prescription drugs to alleviate these obesity-related diseases is firmly addressed.

It is time to demarcate fact from fiction, as it pertains to the sad reality of the American health status — as a whole. Childhood obesity is a multi-factorial issue combining environmental factors such as family, school, peers, community leaders, media, one's own mental perception, and motivation in combination with heredity. A support system that consistently encourages an overweight/obese child to eat nutritious foods and exercise regularly is a bulk of the solution, but does not solve the problem entirely.

How far have today's children tipped the scale?

The prevalence of overweight and obese children has rapidly increased in the past two to three decades. The number of overweight children of 2-5 years old has increased 5.0% to 12.4%; for those aged 6–11 years, prevalence increased from 6.5% to 17.0%; and for those aged 12–19 years, prevalence increased from 5.0% to 17.6%, according to the National Health and Nutrition Examination Survey — taken in 1976-1980 and repeated in 2003-2006 (CDC, 2009).

Childhood obesity is quickly becoming the world's most prevalent nutritional disorder. Many of the associated risks for developing early onset of various adult diseases pose a serious threat to the future of this world. Approximately 60% of overweight children and adolescents have at least one additional risk factor for cardiovascular disease. Awareness concerning this issue is necessary because for the first time, there is an unfortunate possibility that this generation of children may not live as long as their parents in terms of life span (Dietz, 2001).

A society filled with opportunities just a click away and food available on the run contribute to this growing trend of obesity. Currently, over 9 million children in the United States are classified as obese. Although only 25-30% of obesity in adults in the United States begins during childhood or adolescence, early childhood overweight that continues into adulthood renders severe, dangerous obesity among adults (Dietz, 2001).

Researchers clearly state that some children are at an elevated risk for becoming overweight adults. Children who have overweight biological parents are twice as likely to become overweight in adulthood, as are children with normal-weighted parents (Dietz, 1994).

We are aware that this has rapidly exploded as an epidemic in today's society based on this historical research conducted some 20-30 years ago comparing that generation of children and adult's physical and mental wellness states to today's children and adult's physical and mental wellness states.

The gene pool within the country has not changed substantially over the past 20 years. Only environmental effects on energy balance can account for the incidence of overweight children. These increases were consistent among all ages, genders, and ethnicities considered. Key mechanisms include modifications in the balance of dietary intake and physical activity levels of children (affirmed by the two National Health Examination Surveys).

Factors for this burgeoning crisis

The underlying assumptions that can be proposed are that American's eating habits and overall lifestyle, per se, have drastically taken a turn for the worse. Over the last 20 to 30 years, many technological breakthroughs have allowed us to accomplish more things in a quicker span of time. Society has suddenly become fast-paced and highly competitive. Many individuals no longer see the need to do anything "the old fashioned way" — through long hours of diligence and patience. Immediate gratification has become the means to satisfy much of our nutritional wants and needs through the over consumption of fast food.

The fast food industry has an outstanding effect on the psyche of obese individuals. These people have control problems as it is and they desire something readily available, easily digestible, and in large amounts. Another factor involved is the family's socioeconomic status. It is expensive to eat healthy foods on a consistent basis. People who cannot afford these products tend to get quick and easy, less healthy foods — at a lower price (McMurray, 2000).

Sitting down to enjoy a home cooked meal has become less popular in today's society. Food portions have escalated to all-time highs where the "waste not, want not" adage for eating our daily meals has surfaced and become the trend. All-you-can eat buffets and sit-down entrees are, often times, inviting in terms of their affordable prices for the hefty portions of the meal provided. We are a society that wants the most for our dollar and we are consuming the "food" product today much more than we ever have in history.

The media has impacted youth in many different facets that contribute to a more sedentary lifestyle. Watching television, playing on the computer, and playing video games are very popular activities among youth — that reinforce a less-than-active lifestyle (Rideout et al., 2005).

Under the "No Child Left Behind Act", there is a greater academic demand on the students than there ever was in our history and less of a stipulate for physical activity in school — often times not even being assessed as a grade at various schools in the U.S. The amount of physical activity during the course of a day has declined markedly due to the national standards impressed upon school districts throughout the United States. When the students complete their school day and come home, in many instances, they are not given free time for a couple of hours to run about and play in the neighborhood. Events are more structured and centered on the parents' schedules. It turns out that exercise is good for learning, as well as having a positive effect on anxiety, depression, ADHD, addiction, hormonal imbalances, and aging (Ratey, 2008).

The right kinds of questions that we should be asking to solve this problem

- What are the long-term physical, social, and emotional consequences resulting from childhood obesity?

- What are schools, families, and communities doing to curb this growing epidemic in society today?

- What early intervention methods/strategies can be taken to help prevent harmful, life-long negative effects from childhood obesity?

The National Education Association Today has focused its attention on the growth of America's children, not in terms of height, but rather girth, and how poorer cognitive skills, higher anxiety levels, and problems with hyperactivity and attention spans have resulted. The National Association of State Boards of Education and the Institute of Medicine report a growing number of children at risk and suffering from being overweight/obese. The contents of many vending machines at schools is a contributor to this problem and how health experts say that these sugary and fatty foods contradict the efforts to improve breakfast and lunch choices in the cafeteria (Crute, 2005).

Teachers and other support professionals are taking a stand and offering creative, healthy ways of living for students during the course of the school day. While budget is always a concern in the minds of district representatives, a need for physical and mental wellness is beginning to take precedence.

Obesity-linked illnesses are sending a growing number of today's youth to the doctor's offices and hospitals. It is mentioned that many of these children's families do not have the health insurance coverage and cannot afford to get any treatment. The resulting effects can be detrimental to the overall learning of the student (Schneider and Brill, 2005).

Outside of nutrition and exercise, surgical procedures are used as a viable treatment for obesity. Bariatric surgery is a popular method of treatment — primarily for adults that require it and can afford it (Brolin, 2004). Identifying potential risks involved and the benefits are necessary for those considering this procedure for a child. The need for access to counseling services is something that should be taken into account prior to making a decision of this magnitude.

European efforts to combat this pandemic

The epidemic of childhood obesity has risen throughout Europe — as it has in the U.S. According to the WHO Regional Office for Europe, almost 400 million individuals (aged 15 years and older) throughout Europe are estimated to be overweight. Obesity is estimated to affect approximately 130 million adults (Knai et al., 2007; WHO, 2006). About 30% of European children are overweight, and approximately one quarter of them are obese (Knai et al., 2007; Wang and Lobstein, 2006). Overweight and obesity in most countries of Europe reveal rising secular trends and are predicted to continue increasing, if not dealt with appropriately (Knai et al., 2007).

British citizens are among the worst in fighting this epidemic. The government launched campaigns to encourage people, especially youth, to take responsibility for their lives. They looked into providing vouchers for fruit and vegetable purchases as a social marketing strategy to battle this epidemic. The World Health Organization (WHO) launched a global strategy on diet and physical activity after health ministers from across the globe approved the plan. The European Union (EU) outlined plans for addressing the marketing of unhealthy products to children, policy initiatives in agriculture, education, and transportation to address this problem (WHO, 2006).

The obesity pandemic serves as the greatest public health challenge of this century for Europeans. School lunch menus, for the most part, are poorly regulated and contain little nutritional value. The Western cultural influence has overtaken a vast majority of the European society and to some degree has influenced past meal customs of sitting down to eat small portions in a family setting. Children are targeted by television commercials to consume sugary drinks and fast foods high in sugar and fat (Crawford, 1999). Early intervention methods to help counteract the epidemic are discussed.

Family-based approaches for obesity prevention

Efforts are being made to alter a growing number of parents' beliefs, attitudes, knowledge, and practices regarding feeding their children and regulating the time spent playing video games, playing on the computer, and watching television. As it pertains to food choices made, family practices affect the actual food choices, preparation, and consumption. For instance, the Hispanic culture prides itself on eating rice and beans on a consistent basis, while many Italians consume pasta dishes (high carbohydrate content). Portion sizes and consumption of meals vary among different cultures. Many families prepare with cream, butter, margarine, or high fat cheeses that contribute to poor eating habits on a daily basis (Katz, 2004).

Foods that are calorie-dense and potential sources of excess caloric intake that could lead to obesity include regular milk, sugar-sweetened beverages, high-fat foods, and fast foods. Likewise, eating fruits, vegetables, and whole grains may satiate the appetite, due to the fiber content in many of these foods and offset high-calorie intake. Children that eat sit down meals with their families tend to consume more fruits and vegetables and less sugary drinks and fried foods. If parents set stricter guidelines to when and where for consumption of food, better choices tend to be made by children. Also, choosing to breastfeed babies, rather than formula feed them, may prevent subsequent obesity (Dietz, 2001).

The psychological approach that parents have to their children's eating habits is important. In young children, if parents restrict access to various foods, then that appears to increase the preference for those foods. On the other hand, encouraging children to eat may decrease the intake of that particular food offered. Lastly, parental efforts to control the amount of food consumed by children are associated with impaired regulation of caloric intake (Johnson and Birch, 1994).

Families can also encourage more physical activity through performing chores around the house, taking the family dog for a walk and encouraging safe outdoor play with siblings and/or friends, if possible. However, the world today is certainly not the world of many years ago in terms of the nature of neighborhoods. Crime rates continue to pose a threat to many neighborhoods and prevent children from getting sufficient outdoor activity. Many parents in big cities look for ways to get their children outside more often (McMurray, 2000). Sending them to do errands remains a common task that parents ask of their children. Nowadays, young people must proceed with caution in the streets. In my opinion, these factors have contributed to the understated importance of sports participation by youth. However, there are not any studies to date that have statistically documented the relative contribution of organized sports for children to having a healthy lifestyle.

Primary intervention needs to begin very early on in a child's life from the moment of birth. Primary health care providers offer guidance counselors that can assist parents to increase their knowledge base as it pertains to a healthy family lifestyle (Dietz, 2001).

The counselor's focus should be on proper food intake strategies, restrictions for the amount of time watching television, and the amount of physical activity. Television and computer time affect both food intake and energy levels of the child. This is a challenge for many working parents who may not possess complete control over the amount of media viewing. Rather, when parents are home, they can set restrictions and remain consistent for the amount of "tube time." If this time is deprived even so much where a child does not have a television or computer in her/his room, then the choice of physical activity may be more favorably perceived versus a parent requiring a child to be more active (Crawford, 1999). Nonetheless, the division of responsibility between parents and children offers another potential intervention point for health care counseling.

Tips for parents to help children be healthy

- Practice what you preach. Be a good role model.

- Instill good habits and values in your children from birth.

- Keep healthy foods in the house.

- Encourage your children to stay active and engage in playing sports.

- Monitor their friends and how they entertain themselves.

- Communicate with your health care provider, school monitors, and baby sitters.

- Have family dinners and breakfast on a regular basis.

- Involve your children in planning and preparing meals.

- Involve the whole family in activities.

Here is a list of questions to ask yourself (the parent) to see whether you are setting your child up for SUPER HEALTH success.

"To Ask Yourself" Questions:

- ✓ What foods do you have in the house?

- ✓ What foods do you eat daily?

- ✓ What message do you tell your child about food?

- ✓ Do you encourage your child to engage in regular physical activity?

- ✓ How much physical activity do you get?

- ✓ What limits do you impose for computer/video game/television usage?

- ✓ Do you monitor your child's friends?

- ✓ Are you and your child's other parent on the same SUPER HEALTH page?

✓ Do you ask for your child's input about healthy foods she/he would enjoy eating regularly?

✓ Do you support a daily routine for your child so she/he can work towards SUPER HEALTH?

Potential long-term physical, social, and emotional consequences resulting from childhood obesity

Studies have examined the relationship of obesity with such physical, social, and emotional issues. With pediatric obesity increasing at such an alarming rate, one must truly take into consideration the ramifications that this will have for both these individuals that suffer with this condition and those directly or indirectly involved in their lives. Currently, over 60% of the citizens in many first world countries, including the United States, are classified as overweight. This translates to an estimated 3-7 year loss on lifespan and an increase in medical spending on medications and surgeries. Medicare reports that as much as $93 billion dollars was spent due to overweight and obesity conditions ($1400 per person every year) (McCafferty, 2005).

Factors associated with increased obesity prevalence include (Dietz, 1998):

- Increasing age,
- Low activity levels,
- Unstructured family environment,
- Low education levels,
- Smoking,
- Alcohol consumption,
- Glucose intolerance,
- Genetics.

Some possible health effects from being overweight include (Jonides et al., 2002):

- Hypertension,
- High cholesterol levels,

- Venous stasis ulcers,
- Diabetes (type 2),
- Cancer (different types),
- Arthritis,
- Gout,
- Sex-hormone abnormalities,
- Non-alcoholic steatohepatitis.

Overweight children are also more likely to have broken bones and joint problems and this poses a double negative because musculoskeletal pain, often times, leads to reduced mobility and agility and possibly to less physical activity. Psychological issues can result from long-standing obesity such as poor self-esteem, depression, eating disorders, and family dynamics (Jonides et al., 2002).

Solutions to downsize the "SUPERSIZED" generation

Finding solutions has been the primary focus for many years now. In short, it has been clearly stated that a well-balanced diet and sufficient exercise help children grow and develop properly. In reality, the issue is not all that simple as we can see. Obesity is a multi-factorial issue and what may be helpful for one child may not work for another. The proper message must be given to children, on a consistent basis, from all reaches of adult life. Adults are responsible for either helping or hurting a child's healthy development.

PARENTS CAN…

- Plan healthy activities where the whole family can participate. Examples include taking after dinner walks, weekend walks, bicycle rides, or some form of aerobic exercise. The U.S. Surgeon General recommends that children get at least 60 minutes a day of some form of aerobic activity to maintain a high metabolism (USDHHS, 2000).

- Set restrictions on time spent in front of a computer, television, and other multi-media participation.

- Moderate food portions. Children should be fed consistent meals and snacks at regular intervals. Eating at least one meal a day together as a family is important and this is a great time to introduce new, healthy foods into a child's diet. Breakfast time is very important for a child. Brain foods such as oatmeal, eggs, high protein cereals, and fruits are good choices to help children get off to a good start in meeting their nutritional needs.

- Get a child involved in the decision-making process for eating healthy. Provide a menu of healthy food choices for a meal or allow a child to help create a menu filled with healthy food choices.

- Schedule daily active chores for a child to accomplish.

- Help develop a strategy to create an activity program for children (if the community or school system does not support or is unable to afford athletic programs). One can start by asking her/his child to ask her/his friends what their favorite sporting activities include. From there, one can locate a play area and schedule a day or two that works for other parents that can help supervise. This would be a fabulous way to get an overweight child involved in a physical activity. Activities that are non-competitive can be best — such as walking in the woods, bicycling as a group, or flying a kite.

- Find out what a child enjoys that is active and encourage that aspect. This is important for fostering a child's interest in physical activity.

SCHOOLS CAN…

- Promote healthy eating at lunchtime by providing nutritious products for the development of food preference.

- Allow more time for physical activity throughout the day — while maintaining the curriculum standards for the core subjects.

- Find more ways to implement nutritional education into classrooms.

TEACHERS CAN...

- Eat healthy foods in front of children during lunch (if allowed to).

- Offer incentives for students to live healthy.

- Break for stretching, squatting, or jumping in place to rejuvenate students on a stressful day.

- Assign wellness projects where students work cooperatively to track their activity and meals daily. They could be held accountable for their actions through peer signatures as an attest to completing their "wellness project."

- Take the class to the café as an educational lesson to learn about healthy eating. A field trip to a local grocery store reading labels and choosing healthy foods can be very well suited as a life-long skill.

FOOD SERVICE WORKERS CAN...

- Encourage children to choose fresh fruits and vegetables to eat, and water to drink by setting up attractive advertisements and/or colorful displays, rather than eating fried foods and drinking sodas.

- Keep a salad bar well stocked and neat, thus enticing children to make healthy choices.

- Speak to children about positive effects that healthy food choices provide, as opposed to less healthy choices.

- Prepare food by using extra virgin olive oil or by baking/grilling, as opposed to frying foods.

COMMUNITY LEADERS CAN…

- Enforce health policies by seeing all factors that influence childhood obesity and how their decisions can either adversely or positively affect children.

Further research on food consumption should be studied. Does obesity stem from overeating, undereating, and consuming larger portioned meals at the wrong times of the day or is genetics the overriding factor here?

Researching the topic of motivation is important for the success of a child beyond just improving her/his physical appearance. In severe situations of apathy demonstrated by an obese child, have a discussion or schedule a visit for a child to see a licensed practitioner (psychologist or psychiatrist) as to what the barriers to exercise are personally for that individual and what can be done to overcome these barriers. This can be the first step to improve motivation and the will to take a stand on one's health.

Playing with friends is less intimidating than playing with other children that are unfamiliar. Lastly, if all of the methods that attempted fail to make a marked difference on a child, speak with a pediatrician before trying any drastic weight reduction program. Specialized experts can rule out any possible rare medical conditions and then safely put a child on a weight loss plan.

Many obese people in this world have tried desperately to lose weight by exercising and cutting calories, but have found temporary, limited, or no success. Whether the attempt was valiant or not is irrelevant; it just did not work for them. It is, often times, ingrained in their heads that they are victims of poor genetics and that there is nothing that can be done to solve the problem.

Further research into the power of the mind and belief of a higher power to help guide an individual to become successful would be highly beneficial. Looking beyond hereditary or socio-economics and learning how to become one with thyself and gaining a deeper spiritual essence of the individual, in relation to the world, can help one become wiser and more self-disciplined in the midst of crisis. Ingrained, deep-rooted beliefs can ultimately determine one's health or lack thereof.

When the perception of ourselves changes from a superficial, materialistic basis to a more spiritual basis, we begin to understand our true power within. This spiritual approach may prove to change one's view on "impossible." One's eating habits can change along with the desire to become more courageous in the face of societal adversity. Challenges can seem endless, but hope is infinite.

Over the years as a teacher, I have witnessed the effects of childhood obesity in the classroom. It was not my position to discuss this matter with them personally, as they were probably well aware, at their age, that they had a problem controlling their weight. Rather, peer interaction, participation, and overall academic motivation in the classroom are factors that I viewed through my own perspective.

Childhood obesity is a growing epidemic in today's society without any clear-cut solutions provided to help decrease its prevalence. Growing up, I experienced various forms of bullying quite often for different reasons and I have seen overweight/obese children suffer through similar situations that were unwarranted. I have noticed the daily agonies that obese individuals have to deal with both mentally and physically. For children to have this additional burden in their lives poses quite a challenge and puts them at an unfair disadvantage for achieving their goals. The implications are that parents have the most influential role in the war on childhood obesity. Family structure largely contributes to the making or breaking of a lifestyle plan.

> **"More than ever, we as parents and a nation must do something about the growth of obesity in our children. We must do more than just talk, we must be concerned enough to act."**

> **-LEE HANEY**
> **(former 8- time Mr. Olympia bodybuilding champion)**

Chapter IV
A MESSAGE FOR THOSE WHO CARE

"Passion rebuilds the world for the youth. It makes all things alive and significant."

-RALPH WALDO EMERSON
(poet, philosopher)

The Golden Rules To Follow For A Child's Success

❑ A child's lasting behaviors start with YOU! Violence besets violence. Acts of kindness and caring bring forth trust and respect.

❑ Get involved and remain active in a child's life. Do not be afraid to set the boundaries that children expect and deep-down long for from you.

❑ Frequently bring up the topics of school, friends, relationships, and hobbies, keeping lines of communication always open.

Life is filled with trials, tribulations, and plenty of discoveries. Having fun and being excited about life are important parts of living well. To define fun and provide further insights, we need to frame the context appropriately — whether it is at school, with family, with friends, at home, being alone, dating, etc. Allowing children to "just be kids and have fun" have various connotations among people. People may view that young people seek instant gratification all of the time, expecting things always to be fun and exciting, rather than gaining a sense of long-term enjoyment and fulfillment. Other people view that children's definition of fun is "risky, violent, or very intense."

The state of being in constant acceleration and preparation for the future has become the modality for raising children in our country. There is becoming a widespread incorporation of "educational" pieces attributed to many aspects of school curricula. The increasing number of assessments that children are required to take throughout their schooling life is in large part due to the "No Child Left Behind (NCLB) Act." Educators make efforts to engage children in educationally exciting and meaningful curricula —which help foster good, productive citizens.

Student participation in school activities is a key motivator to increase a child's engagement at school. Researchers have found that participation levels at school decrease as the class size increases. The National Longitudinal Study of Adolescent Health conducted this research using a sample of 14,966 students in 84 schools and researchers concluded that students felt more detached from their school and to their teachers. They also concluded that students' participation in extracurricular activities diminished at a steady rate as school size increased (Crosnoe et al., 2004). The patterns found in the study did not differ on the race and/or ethnicity of the student.

This study suggests that interpersonal relationships are very important for the social well-being of an individual and fosters greater participation and motivation at school. Even at schools where there are large student populations, students may benefit from a large number and variety of opportunities in clubs and/or teams. Creating smaller settings in a large school can also help teacher-student relationships, increase the actual learning time, help better recognize individual student needs, and provide a safer environment for learning to take place.

Going to physical education class is becoming an education in the sense that discussions are now including topics on stress management, nutrition, weight training, and other life-long activities. The days of rolling out a cart of balls and setting up teams to play games are becoming a thing of the past. While this method of physically educating children may have been aerobic, it certainly was not the most inclusive strategy to get everyone active.

Project Adventure, the nation's first "Adventure Curriculum for Physical Education," has been designed for elementary and secondary education to improve a child's physical well-being as well as to build confidence, patience, teamwork, acceptance, and trust. The lesson plans are comprised of collaborative, cooperative activities that focus on developing leadership ability, social competency, conflict resolution skills, and problem-solving skills. The skills learned in this program have been seen by teachers in other disciplines and have translated into a positive learning behavior and attitude. Students seek out challenges, self-advocate, and demonstrate more confidence and leadership in the classroom (Project Adventure, 2008).

Understanding the big picture to what it is that we truly desire from children is the most important factor. Here are some specific ways in which all adults can demonstrate and reinforce the concept to "JUST BE."

- Take time to separate work from play and have an optimistic point of view about life. Painting the picture as positive is a strong message that we can give children by showing it in our own daily routines at work, at home, and in association with others in society.

- Being a life-long learner and keeping an open mind to new and exciting things show a child that there is a great deal to learn and look forward to in life. Having a thirst for knowledge and curiosity is what makes things very special for a youngster.

- Keep an open-minded approach to all facets of life and encourage a child to participate in many different activities. The more activities exposed to a child, the greater long-term fulfillment and joy amassed.

- Be young and enjoy yourself, your family, and your friends by balancing work with pleasure. Do not be afraid to try something out of your own comfort zone that may result in making you look silly. This is a great message for a child: "Don't be afraid to fail!"

- Participate in an activity with a child. Take advantage of many different outdoor and indoor activities such as organized sports, bike riding, jogging, weight training, ice-skating, skiing, dancing, and/or educational games on the computer.

❑ Your actions dictate what a child learns from you such as:

➤ Problem-solving strategies.

➤ Anger management techniques.

➤ Responses to stressful situations.

➤ Respect in a relationship.

➤ Impulsive control.

➤ Tolerance and patience toward others.

➤ Cultural openness to others.

We have heard of Albert Einstein's Law of Relativity and how the value of the energy of a physical system is equivalent to the product of its mass and the speed of light squared ($E = mc^2$). The understanding of this law may or may not be a priority unless that is your specialization as a quantum physicist and/or you relish in being an avid fan of Mr. Einstein. The analogy to be made and understood here is that one's energy is like the universe's energy — infinite and limitless. Hence, it is there for one to draw upon and direct in whatever so called manner one chooses. One's intentions (mass) multiplied by one's direct actions (speed of light) can generate a positive or negative result in one's character.

You have the POWER! Be active in a child's life!

Chapter V

A Message To The Beloved Child Within All Of Us

"The individual has always had to struggle to keep from being overwhelmed by the tribe. If you try it, you will be lonely often, and sometimes frightened. But no price is too high to pay for the privilege of owning yourself."

- FRIEDRICH NIETZSCHE
(philosopher)

Behaving responsibly may be difficult and often times a sacrifice throughout life. You may have to give something of yourself and get nothing in return or worse yet, wounded in the process, but each gift that you give to something in this world is another token deposited into the SUPER POWER account. Just ask Spider-Man, "With great power comes great responsibility!" This is both a gift and a curse. Giving of yourself from time-to-time and neglecting your own personal desires are what those who care most for you always do.

As you get older, you have to make more and more decisions about your life. You will be wracked with doubt and indecision along the way, making mistakes and not quite sure of where you may be going. One day, you may want to save the world and rid it from disease. Suddenly, you wake up the next day and decide that dealing with blood is not your cup of tea, but inspiring children and becoming a teacher is. Time elapses further and you decide that kids drive you crazy so you declare that having your own business is your calling. This is completely normal and life is full of these kinds of choices. Keep in mind that every decision that you make in your life will impact your overall mental and physical wellness to a certain degree.

Speaking to an elderly man in a wheelchair at a basketball park the summer entering into my senior year of high school on a warm summer day taught me the most valuable lesson on health and appreciation of life that I recall to this day. The handicapped elderly man spoke to me at the end of the game when I walked off the court dejected from losing and said to me, "Good game kid. You really gave it your all out there!" I remarked saying, "Yeah, but we lost. Today was a bad day." He replied, "You know young man, EVERY DAY is a GOOD day, but some days are better than others. Look at you. You are young and healthy. Who could ask for anything more? Thankfully, some things you don't have to think about like I do each day, like millions of people do each day. Let me tell you something to remember, kid, and never forget this…

MY HEALTH IS VERY VALUABLE TO ME……. BECAUSE I LOST IT! I SEE THE GOOD IN LIFE NOW AND THOSE HAVE BECOME MY THOUGHTS….MY ONLY THOUGHTS. *SAVE YOURSELF NOW, KID!* CHERISH EACH MOMENT THAT YOU ARE ALIVE AND VALUE YOUR LIFE!"

From that moment forth, I saw life through different eyes. I became much more appreciative to the meaning and beauty that could be found in each moment everyday. Everything that happens in life is AMAZING and for a reason, not all of it good or bad, but nonetheless remarkable. The lesson to be learned is to appreciate what you do have and relish it for the moment in time. Focus on the good experiences in life and process out any fears, anger, rage, and/or disappointment that you may have and you will remain young at heart and stay clear of becoming a bitter, angry old person one day. Stay healthy by doing the right things.

Appreciate what you have and work to make it that much better. Do not take for granted what could be lost in a blink of an eye. Learn from other people's mistakes and words of wisdom. We don't have to personally experience the dark to see and be the light. We don't have to wait for our busy lives to be interrupted with tragedy to hear nature and the silence breathe life's essence. It is YOUR decision to make because ultimately…it is YOUR LIFE!

If you do not get what you feel you deserve or yearn right away, step back a moment and see if it is what your heart desires for the right reasons. If your mind and heart are one in the same, then go for it! Don't worry about failure because there is really no such thing. That is nothing more than a perception. There is no such thing unless you give up on life. The human being has an amazing ability to adapt to changing situations in order to survive. Once adapted and evolved, then it will be time for you to be free!

You may have heard your parents or teachers mention on at least one occasion how "one bad apple can spoil the whole bunch." If you have ever eaten a bad apple before, you realize that you indeed feel the ill effects afterwards. Sometimes there are worms or smaller parasites that get into the apple that cause the breakdown. Protect yourself by surrounding yourself around positive energy, not to be confused with necessarily "popular" energy that may suck the life from you, like a parasite, and strip your identity.

For today's youth, you will develop friendships early on that may last a lifetime and you will share many memories together. Choose friends who are encouraging, motivating, and full of life. You will feed off each other and become quite similar in many ways. When you feel down, a true friend is there to help rebuild your spirits by listening, understanding, and encouraging. Demonstrate that genuine care toward others and you will be amazed at what you will attract in your life beyond friendships. A wise man once said to me, "Your true character is how you behave when you think nobody is watching you." How true that is!

The Golden Rules For Youth To Follow

❑ Treat your family, friends, and others with the utmost of respect.

- ❑ Work to the best of your ability and do your homework regularly.

- ❑ Give 100% work ethic.

- ❑ Eat healthy (as often as possible).

- ❑ Be physically active.

- ❑ Get good sleep.

- ❑ Help out around the house by performing chores.

- ❑ Be a leader and stand up for others.

- ❑ Say thank you to those who help you along the way.

- ❑ Find a passion and make your dreams come true (It does take discipline and hard work!).

The following message below is directed to the beloved child in ALL OF US. As we can see, change starts from within — one person at a time. Through this example, we can revolutionize the masses and live out our greatest truths. If you successfully proceeded through this book and still feel a sense of disconnect and misunderstood by society, the following famous quote illustrates that you are never alone and can be understood if you choose to let yourself be.

"I AM YOU AND YOU ARE ME AND *WE* ARE *ONE*!"

For all the devoted human beings who truly care to see the child within them attain SUCCESS, let this passage from the chapter on children in *The Prophet* guide you toward your TRUTH:

"And a woman who held a babe against her bosom said, 'Speak to us of Children'.
And he said: Your children are not your children. They are the sons and daughters of Life's longing for itself.

They come through you but not from you,
And though they are with you, yet they belong not to you.
You may give them your love but not your thoughts.
For they have their own thoughts.
You may house their bodies but not their souls,
For their souls dwell in the house of tomorrow, which you cannot
visit, not even in your dreams.
You may strive to be like them, but seek not to make them like
you.
For life goes not backward nor tarries with yesterday.
You are the bows from which your children as living arrows are
sent forth.
The archer sees the mark upon the path of the infinite, and He
bends you with His might that His arrows may go swift and far.
Let your bending in the archer's hand be for gladness;
For even as He loves the arrow that flies, so he loves also the bow
that is stable."

-KAHLIL GIBRAN
(poet, artist, philosopher)

REFERENCES

Altabe, M. (1998). Ethnicity and body image: Quantitative and qualitative analysis. *International Journal of Eating Disorders*, 23: 153-9.

American Council on Science and Health, Inc. <u>Cigarettes: What the Warning Label Doesn't Tell You—Information Tobacco Companies Don't Want Teens to Know About the Dangers of Smoking.</u> United States: American Council on Science and Health, Inc., 2003.

American Psychiatric Association. (2006). Treatment of patients with eating disorders, third edition.

American Psychiatric Association. *Am J Psychiatry*, 163(7 Suppl): 4-54.

Anderson, T. Every Officer is a Leader: Coaching Leadership, Learning and Performance in Justice, Public Safety, and Security Organizations. United States: Trafford Publishing, 2006.

Apuzzo, M. (2007, April 19). Epitaph of a madman. *Republican-American*, p. 4A.

Aseltine, R.H., Jr., and R.C. Kessler. (1993). Marital disruption and depression in a community sample. *Journal of Health and Social Behavior*, 34(Sep.): 237-251.

Bandura A & R.H. Walters. (1963). Social learning and personality development. New York: Holt, Rinehart & Winston, 329 p. [Stanford Univ., Stanford, CA and Univ. Waterloo, Ontario, Canada].

Barlow, S., W.H. Dietz, W.J. Klish, and F.L. Trowbridge. (2002). Medical Evaluation of Overweight Children and Adolescents. *Pediatrics*, 110(1): 222-229.

Belekeviciute, L. (2007). Bachelor's Paper- <u>Anorexia Nervosa In Sociological Perspective: The Factors For the Emergence of Illness and Patients' Personal Experiences.</u>

Benokraitis, N. <u>Marriages & Families: Changes, Choices, and Constraints.</u> New Jersey: Pearson Prentice Hall, 2008.

Berkman ND, Lohr KN, Bulik CM. (2007). Outcomes of eating disorders: a systematic review of the literature. *Int J Eat Disord.*, 40(4): 293-309.

Brolin, R. (2004). Bariatric Surgery and long term control of morbid obesity. *Journal of the American Medical Association*, 288 (22): 2793-2796.

Cawley, J., C. Meyerhoefer, and D. Newhouse. (2006). Not your father's PE: Obesity, exercise, and the role of schools. *Education Next*, 1, 60-66.

Chao, R. K. (1994). Beyond parental control and authoritarian parenting style: Understanding Chinese parenting through the cultural notion of training. *Child Development*, 65(4), 1111-1119.

Collins, R., and S. Coltrane Sociology of Marriage and the Family: Gender, Love, and Property. United States: Wadsworth Publishing, 2000.

Crawford, D.A. (1999). Television viewing, physical inactivity and obesity. *International Journal of Obesity*, 23: 437-440.

Crosnoe, R., M. Kirkpatrick Johnson, and G.H. Elder, Jr. (2004). School Size and the Interpersonal Side of Education: An Examination of Gender and Organizational Context." *Social Science Quarterly* 85(5), 1259-1274.

Crute, S. (2005, March). Growing Pains. *NEA Today*, 23, 23-31.

Darling, N., and L. Steinberg. (1993). Parenting style as context: An integrative model. *Psychological Bulletin*, 113(3), 487-496.

Davies, B. Becoming male or female. Jackson, S., and S. Scott (eds.) Gender: A Sociological Reader. New York: Routledge, 2002, pgs. 85-110.

Dietz, W.H. (2004). Overweight in childhood and adolescence. *New England Journal of Medicine*, 350 (9): 855-857.

Dietz, W.H. (2001). Relationship of Childhood Obesity to Coronary Heart Disease Risk Factors in Adulthood: The Bogalusa Heart Study. *Pediatrics*, 108(3): 712-719.

Dietz, W.H. (1998). Health consequences of obesity in youth: childhood predictors of adult disease. *Pediatrics*, 101: 518-525.

Dietz, W.H., (1994). Critical periods in childhood for the development of obesity. *American Journal of Clinical Nutrition*, 59: 955-959.

Farias, M. 25 Ways to Keep Your Child Safe, Happy and Successful: Lessons from a School Counselor. Canada: Trafford Publishing, 2007.

Fergusson, D.M., J.M. Boden, and L.J. Horwood. (2007). Recurrence of major depression in adolescence and early adulthood, and later mental health, educational and economic outcomes. *The British Journal of Psychiatry*, 191: 335-342.

Findlay, L., and A. Bowker. (2007). The Link between Competitive Sports Participation and Self-Concept in Early Adolescence: A Consideration of Gender and Sport Orientation. *J Youth Adolescence*, 38: 29-40.

Furstenberg, F.F., and K.E. Kiernan. (2001). Delayed parental divorce: How much do children benefit? *Journal of Marriage and Family* 63(May): 446-457.

Gardner, H. Leading Minds: An Anatomy Of Leadership. United States. The Perseus Books Group, 1995.

Giddens, A. Sociology. Cambridge: Polity Press, 2001.

Gidwani, G.P. and E.S. Rome. (1997). Eating Disorders. *Clinical Obstetrics and Gynecology*, 40(3), 601- 615.

Gilligan, J. Preventing Violence. New York: Thames & Hudson, 2001.

Gilligan, J. (2003). Shame, Guilt, and Violence. *Social Research* 70(4): 1149.

Giordano, S. Understanding Eating Disorders. Oxford University Press, 2005.

Grall, T.S. (2003). Custodial mothers and fathers and their child support: 2001. U.S. Census Bureau, Current Population Reports, P60-225.

Grant, B., and D. Dawson. (1997). Age at Onset of Alcohol Use and Its Association with DSM-IV Alcohol Abuse and Dependence. Results from the National Longitudinal Alcohol Epidemiologic Survey. *Journal of Substance Abuse*, 9: 103-110.

Hammer, H., D. Finkelhor, and A.J. Sedlak. (2002). Children Abducted by Family Members: National Estimates and Characteristics. *National Incidence Studies of Missing, Abducted, Runaway, and Thrownaway Children*. Washington, DC: U.S. Department of Justice, Office of Justice Programs, Office of Juvenile Justice and Delinquency Prevention.

Heaney, R., M. Dowell, K. Rafferty, and J. Bierman. (2000). Bioavailability of the calcium in fortified soy imitation milk, with some observations on method. *Am J Clin Nutr.*, 71: 1166-1169.

Hetherington, E.M., and J. Kelly. (2002). *For better or for worse: Divorce reconsidered*. New York: W.W. Norton.

Hill, N. Think And Grow Rich. New York: The Random House Publishing Group, 1937.

Hoffman, J.P. (2006). Extracurricular Activities, Athletic Participation, and Adolescent Alcohol Use: Gender-Differentiated and School-Contextual Effects. *Journal of Health and Social Behavior*, 47: 275–290.

Holden, M.J. Therapeutic Crisis Intervention. New York: The Family Life Development Center, Fifth Edition, 2001.

Hudson J.I., E. Hiripi, H.G. Pope, and R.C. Kessler. (2007). The prevalence and correlates of eating disorders in the national comorbidity survey replication. *Biological Psychiatry*, 61: 348-358.

James, W.P. (2006). The challenge of childhood obesity. *International Journal of Pediatric Obesity*, 1: 7-10.

Jeffreys, M. Success Secrets of the Motivational Superstars. United States: Prima Lifestyles, 1996.

Jennings, T. (2005, May 19). House approves ban on soda, sugar snacks. *Republican-American*, p. A1.

Johnson, S.L., and L.L. Birch. (1994). Parents' and children's adiposity and eating style. *Pediatrics*, 94: 653–61.

Johnston, L.D., P.M. O'Malley, J.G. Bachman, and J.E. Schulenberg. (2006). *Monitoring the Future National Results on Adolescent Drug Use: Overview of Key Findings, 2005.* (NIH Publication No. 06-5882). Bethesda, MD: National Institute on Drug Abuse.

Jonides, L., V. Buschbacher, and S. Barlow. (2002). Management of Child and Adolescent Obesity: Psychological, Emotional, and Behavioral Assessment. *Pediatrics*, 110 (1): 215-221.

Katz, S. (ed) <u>Encyclopedia Of Food And Culture</u>. United States: Gale Group and Thomson Learning, Inc., 2004.

Kiess, W., A. Böttner, K. Raile, T. Kapellen, G. Müller, A. Galler[a], R. Paschke, and M. Wabitsch. (2003). Type 2 Diabetes mellitus in Children and Adolescents. *Horm Res.*, 59 (Suppl. 1): 77-84.

Kimmel, M. <u>Masculinity As Homophobia Fear, Shame, and Silence In the Construction of Gender Identity</u>, Brod, H.., and M. Kaufman. (eds.) <u>Theorizing Masculinities</u>. 1994, pgs. 227-241.

King, V. (1994). Variation in the consequences of non-resident father involvement for children's well- being. *Journal of Marriage and the Family*, 56 (Nov.): 953-972.

Knai, C., M. Suhrcke, and T. Lobstein. (2007). Obesity in Eastern Europe: An overview of its health and economic implications. *Economics and Human Biology*, 5: 392-408.

Kohn, A. <u>Punished by Rewards</u>. United States: Mariner Books, 1999.

Krimsky, G., and J. Peck. (2005, June 12). Generation Rx popping pills. *Republican- American*, p.A1.

Leinwand, D. (2006. June 13). Prescription drugs find place in teen culture. *USA Today*.

Males, M. (1999). For Adults, Today's youth are always the worst. *Los Angeles Times*, p.M1.

Mann, A. (1999). Woman's Health Issues and Nuclear Medicine, Part III: Women and Osteoporosis. *The Journal of Nuclear Medicine Technology*, 27: 266-270.

Mauriello, T. (2005, March 16). State's students called the FITTEST. *Republican-American*, p. A1.

McMurray, R.G. (2000). The influence of physical activity, socioeconomic status and ethnicity on the weight status of adolescents. *Obes. Res.*, 8: 130-139.

Miller, P.J., A.R. Wiley, H. Fung, and C.H. Liang. (1997). Personal Storytelling as a Medium of Socialization in Chinese and American Families. *Child Development*, 68: 557-568.

Montenegro, X.P. (2004). *Divorce experience: A study of divorce at midlife and beyond.* Washington, DC: AARP.

National Institute of Mental Health (1982). Television and Behavior: Ten

Years of Scientific Progress and Implications for the Eighties, Volume 1. Rockville, MD: U.S. Department of Health and Human Services.

National Longitudinal Survey of Adolescent Health, Wave II, 1996.

Palm, A.M. War Against the Body: Bulimia and Anorexia from the Perspective of Cultural Sociology, Lundin, S. (eds.) Bodytime: On the Interaction of Body, Identity and Society. Lund University Press, 1997, pgs. 85-110.

Pantley, E. Kid Cooperation: How to Stop Yelling, Nagging and Pleading and Get Kids to Cooperate.California: New Harbinger Publications, 1996."Phobia." *Webster's II New College Dictionary.* 1999 ed.

Pope Jr., H.G., K.A. Phillips, and R. Olivardia. The Adonis Complex: The Secret Crisis of Male Body Obsession. New York: Free Press, 2000.

Ratey, J. Spark: The Revolutionary New Science of Exercise and the Brain. New York: Hatchett Book Group, 2008.

Rector, R.E., K.A. Johnson, and J.A. Marshall. (2004). Teens Who Make Virginity Pledges Have Substantially Improved Life Outcomes. *Center for Data Analysis Report, #04-07.*

Rector, R.E., K.A. Johnson, and L.R. Noyes. (2003). Sexually Active Teenagers Are More Likely to Be Depressed and to Attempt Suicide. *Center for Data Analysis Report, #03-04.*

Rideout, V., D.F. Roberts, and U.G. Foehr. (2005). *Generation M: Media in the lives of 8-18 year-Olds.* Menlo Park, CA: Kaiser Family Foundation.

Sacks J.J.., and D.E. Nelson. (1994). Smoking and injuries: an overview. *Prev Med., 23: 515-20.*

Schneider, M., and S. Brill. (2005). Obesity in Children and Adolescents. *American Academy of Pediatrics,* 26: 155-162.

Schneiderman, N., G. Ironson, and S. Siegel. (2005). Stress and Health: Psychological, Behavioral, and Biological Determinants. *Annu Rev Clin Psychol.,* 1: 607-628.

Schwerin, M.J., and K.J. Corcoran. (1992). What do people think of male steroid users?: An Experimental investigation. *Journal of Applied Social Psychology,* 22 (10): 833.

Shenk, J.W. *Lincoln's Melancholy.* Mariner Books, 2005.

Shilling, C. The Body and Social Theory. London: SAGE, 2003.

Siegel, B. Peace, Love & Healing. New York: HarperCollins Publishers, 1989.

Sothern, M. (2001). Exercise As A Modality In The Treatment Of Childhood Obesity. *Pediatric Clinics of North America,* 48(4), 995-1015.

Stellman, S.D., and K. Resnicow. (1997). Tobacco smoking, cancer and social class. *IARC Scientific* Publications, (138): 229-50.

Stewart, S.D. (1999). Nonresident mothers' and fathers' social contact with children. *Journal of Marriage and the Family.* 61(Nov.): 894-907.

Story, M., and Simone French. (2004). Food Advertising and Marketing

Directed at Children and Adolescents in the US. *International Journal of Behavioral Nutrition and Physical Activity*, 1(3).

Striegel-Moore, R.S. (personal communication, May 2005).

The Henry J. Kaiser Family Foundation and The National Center on Addiction and Substance Abuse at Columbia University, "Millions of Young People Mix Sex with Alcohol or Drugs – With Dangerous Consequences," (2002).

The National Center on Addiction and Substance Abuse (CASA), funded by the Henry J. Kaiser Family Foundation, Dangerous Liaisons: Substance Abuse and Sex (New York: CASA, December 1999).

Thornberry, T.P., C.A. Smith, C. Rivera, D. Huizinga, and M. Stouthamer-Loeber. (1999). *Family disruption and delinquency*. Washington, DC: U.S. Department of Justice, Office of Justice Programs, Office of Juvenile Justice and Delinquency Prevention.

Tombak, M. Can We Live 150 Years? Canada: Healthy Life Press, Inc., 2005.

Unwin, B.K., M.K. Davis, and J.B. DeLeeuw. (2000). Pathologic Gambling. *American Academy of Family Physicians*, 61: 741-749.

U.S. Department of Health and Human Services (2000). *HealthyPeople 2000: National Health Promotion and Disease Prevention Objectives*. Washington, DC: US Department of Health And Human Services, Public Health Services.

U.S. Department of Health and Human Services (1989). Report of the Secretary's Task Force on Youth Suicide, Volume 3: Prevention and Interventions in Youth Suicide, Rockville, MD.

U.S. Department of Health and Human Services. (2007). Substance Abuse and Mental Health Services Administration. Office of Applied Studies. National Survey on Drug Use and Health.

U.S. Department of Health and Human Services. (2004). The Health Consequences of Smoking: A Report of the Surgeon General. U.S. Department of Health and Human Services, Centers for Disease Control and Prevention, National Center for Chronic Disease Prevention and Health Promotion, Office on Smoking and Health.

U.S. Department of Health and Human Services. (2007). The Surgeon General's Call to Action To Prevent and Reduce Underage Drinking. U.S. Department of Health and Human Services, Office of the Surgeon General.

Viner, R.M., and T.J. Cole. (2005). Adult socioeconomic, educational, social, and psychological outcomes of childhood obesity: a national birth cohort study. *British Medical Journal*, 330(7504): 1354- 1366.

Vorath, H.H., & L.K. Brendtro, L.K. Positive Peer Culture (2nd Ed.). New Brunswick: Aldine Transaction, 1985.

Watsford, R. (2008). The success of the 'Pinkie' campaign - Speeding. No one thinks big of you: A new approach to road safety marketing. 2008 Joint ACRS-Travelsafe National Conference – Non-Peer Reviewed Paper.

Weiss, L. H., and J.C. Schwarz. (1996). The relationship between parenting types and older adolescents' personality, academic achievement, adjustment, and substance use. *Child Development*, 67(5), 2101-2114.

WORLD WIDE WEB / INTERNET SOURCES

Preventing Adolescent Suicide. (1996). Retrieved on 28 March 2009. <http://www.ace-network.com/warningsigns.htm>

U.S. EPA. Protecting Children from Pesticides. (2002). Retrieved on 31 March 2009. <http://www.epa.gov/pesticides/factsheets/kidpesticide.htm>

Bidstrup, S. My Child is GAY! Now What Do I Do? (2002). Retrieved on 24 April 2009. <http://www.bidstrup.com/pardata.htm#what>

NASPE. 10 Dec. 2002 <http://www.aahperd.org/naspe/template.cfm?template=pr_121002.html>

Exley, L.R. Beyond Stranger Danger: Teaching Kids How to Avoid Abduction. (2003). Retrieved on 21 April 2009. <http://www.parenthood.com/article-topics/beyond_stranger_danger_teaching_kids_how_to_avoid_abduction.html>

Binge Eating Disorder. (2003). Retrieved on 9 April 2007. <http://www.pbs.org/perfectillusions/eatingdisorders/bingeeating.html>

AAOS: Weight-Bearing Activities May Be Best to Promote Healthy Bone Mass In Adolescent Females. 7 Feb. 2003. <http://www.newswise.com/articles/view/?id=33682>

Henderson, J., G. Henderson, J. Lavikainen and D. McDaid. Actions against depression. (2004). <http://ec.europa.eu/health/ph_determinants/life_style/mental/docs/depression_en.pdf>

National Cancer Institute: 80% of Cancer Cases Due to Environmental & Food Carcinogens. 28 June 2004. <http://www.organicconsumers.org/foodsafety/cancer070104.cfm>

Suicide and Depression. 9 Sept. 2004. <http://www.allaboutdepression.com/gen_04.html>

Dakss, B. Binge Drinking Turning Deadly. 27 Oct. 2004. <http://www.cbsnews.com/stories/2004/10/14/earlyshow/living/parenting/main649375.shtml>

Children and television violence. (2005). *Abelard*. <http://www.abelard.org/tv/tv.php>

Wagner, C. <u>Teens Behind the Wheel.</u> 21 Feb. 2005. <http://www.cpyu. org/Page.aspx?id=163421>

Rasmussen, K. <u>Dilemmas for Parenting Amid the Social Pressures of Eating Disorders.</u> 11 June 2005. <http://www.centerforchange.com/>

Koch, W. <u>'Go-getter,' 18, ousts mayor in Michigan.</u> 13 Nov. 2005. <http:// www.usatoday.com/news/nation/2005-11-09-kid-mayor_x.htm>

Reducing Underage Drinking Through Coalitions (RUDC) Youth and Adults United for Change. 13 Nov. 2005. <http://www.alcoholpolicymd.com/ programs/rudc.htm>

Centers for Disease Control and Prevention (CDC). Web-based Injury Statistics Query and Reporting System (WISQARS). (2005). National Center for Injury Prevention and Control, CDC (producer). <http:// www.cdc.gov/ncipc/wisqars/default.htm>

Robinson, B.A. Professional Associations' statements about Homosexuality. 11 Feb. 2006 <http://www.religioustolerance.org/hom_prof.htm>

Harr, Q. Adolescent Sexual Activity Interrelated With Negative Behaviors. 12 Oct. 2006. <http://www.nationalledger.com/cgi-bin/artman/exec/view. cgi?archive=5&num=9000>

<u>NIAAA: Make a Difference: Talk to Your Child About Alcohol.</u> 24 Oct. 2006 <http://www.collegedrinkingprevention.gov/OtherAlcoholInformation/ makeDifference.aspx>

<u>IFIC: Overweight, Obesity & Weight Management.</u> 15 Nov 2006. <http:// www.ific.org/nutrition/obesity/index.cfm?renderforprint=1>

<u>Leadership Overview.</u> 4 Dec. 2006. <http://www.alcoholfreechildren.org/en/ us/index.cfm#bookmark1>

<u>Boy Scout Aims and Methods.</u> 5 Dec. 2006. <http://www.boyscouttrail. com/>

College Binge Drinking. 5 Dec. 2006. <http://www.drugrehabtreatment. com/collegebingedrinking.html>

WHO, 2006. Obesity in Europe. World Health Organization, Copenhagen. 7 Dec. 2006. <http://www.euro.who.int/obesity>

Mauro, T. <u>Lying vs. "Truthiness": Dealing with dishonesty in children.</u> 18 Feb. 2007. <http://specialchildren.about.com/od/behaviorissues/a/ truthiness.htm>

<u>Youth and Gambling.</u> 19 Feb. 2007. <http://www.mha.sjcg.net/as/gambling/ youth/>

Volkow, N. <u>Marijuana: Facts Parents Need to Know.</u> 20 Feb. 2007. <http:// www.nida.nih.gov/MarijBroch/MarijparentsN.html>

<u>NIDA Research Report Series - Tobacco Addiction.</u> 24 March 2007. <http:// www.drugabuse.gov/researchreports/nicotine/nicotine.html>

Maynard, C. <u>Body Image.</u> 8 April 2007. <http://www.edreferral.com/body_ image.htm>

NEDA: Anorexia Nervosa. 9 April 2007. <http://www.nationaleatingdisorders.
    org>

NEDA: Bulimia Nervosa. 9 April 2007. <http://www.nationaleatingdisorders.
    org>

Lagorio, C. Warning Signs From Student Gunman. 17 April 2007. <http://
    www.cbsnews.com/stories/2007/04/17/eveningnews/main2696236.sht
    ml?source=RSSattr=VirginiaTechTragedy_2696236>

Cullen, D. Psychopath? Depressive? Schizophrenic? Was Cho Seung-Hui
    really like the Columbine killers? 20 April 2007. <http://www.slate.
    com/id/2164757/>

Walsh, D. The malignant resentments that erupted into mass murder in
    Virginia. 20 April 2007. <http://www.wsws.org/articles/2007/apr2007/
    cho-a20.shtml>

Baxter, S. American Psycho. 22 April 2007. <http://www.timesonline.co.uk/
    tol/news/world/us_and_americas/article1686784.ece>

Dornin, R., and A. Reiss. 'Roid rage' questions surround Benoit murder-
    suicide. 29 June 2007. <http://www.cnn.com/2007/US/06/27/wrestler/
    index.html>

Steroid Abuse By School Age Children. 10 July 2007. <http://www.
    deadiversion.usdoj.gov/pubs/brochures/steroids/children/index.html>

AMBER Ready Program. 10 July 2007. <http://www.amberready.com/
    amber_ready.html>

Kreamer, A. Can Your iPod Help You Lose Weight, Reduce Your Blood
    Pressure, and Alleviate Pain? 17 July 2007. <http://health.yahoo.com/
    experts>

NIDA Research Report Series - Marijuana Abuse. 3 Aug. 2007. <http://www.
    drugabuse.gov/PDF/RRMarijuana.pdf>

Fitness For Kids: Helping Kids Learn About Fitness. 20 Aug. 2007. <http://
    orthoinfo.aaos.org/topic.cfm?topic=A00047>

Iannelli, V. Calcium Rich Foods. 29 Oct. 2007. <http://pediatrics.about.
    com/od/calcium/a/06_calcium_food.htm>

New Food Pyramid. 29 Oct. 2007. <http://www.richerlives.com.au/public_
    pages/supersugar.html#healthy>

Kids and Smoking. 10 Nov. 2007. <http://kidshealth.org/parent/positive/
    talk/smoking.html>

Compulsive Exercise. 10 Nov. 2007. <http://kidshealth.org/parent/emotions/
    behavior/compulsive_exercise.html>

Jordan, A.B. (2008). Children's Media Policy. <http://www.futureofchildren.
    org/usr_doc/18_10_Jordan.pdf>

National Institute of Mental Health. (2008). <http://www.nimh.nih.gov/
    health/publications/depression/complete-index.shtml#pub3>

Prescription For Danger: A Report on the Troubling Trend of Prescription and Over-the-Counter Drug Abuse Among the Nation's Teens. 4 Jan. 2008. <http://www.theantidrug.com/pdfs/prescription_report.pdf>

Murad, H. The Key to Supple Skin in the Winter Months. 8 Jan. 2008. <https://www.resurgence.com/resurgence-articles.asp>

TePastte, S. Understanding Major Depression. 28 Jan. 2008. <https://www.messa.org/messa/public/HealthResources/healtharticles/Depression/UnMajorDep.aspx>

NIDA InfoFacts: Drugged Driving. 10 April 2008. <http://www.nida.nih.gov/infofacts/driving.html>

Liptak, A. U.S. prison population dwarfs that of other nations. 23 April 2008. <http://www.iht.com/articles/2008/04/23/america/23prison.php>

NIDA InfoFacts: Steroids (Anabolic-Androgenic). 12 June 2008. <http://www.nida.nih.gov/Infofacts/steroids.html>

National Highway Traffic Safety Administration. 9 July 2008. <http://www.nhtsa.gov/portal/site/nhtsa/menuitem.cd18639c9dadbabbbf30811060008a0c/>

Project Adventure. 14 July 2008. <http://www.pa.org/>

CDC: Alcohol and Public Health. 6 Aug. 2008. < http://www.cdc.gov/alcohol/>

Insurance Institute For Highway Safety. 9 Sept. 2008. <http://www.iihs.org/news/rss/pr090908.html>

Prescription Medicine Abuse: A Serious Problem. 24 Sept. 2008. <http://www.drugfree.org/portal/drugissue/features/prescription_medicine_misuse>

Know Your Child Abduction Facts. 12 Nov. 2008. <http://www.life-prints.com/ChildAbductionPrevention.html>

Possible Causes of Food Allergies. 16 Dec. 2008. <http://www.allergicchild.com/causes_food_allergy.html>

Saisan, J., D. Cutter, and J. Segal. Alcohol Abuse and Alcoholism. 4 Jan. 2009. <http://www.helpguide.org/mental/alcohol_abuse_alcoholism_signs_effects_treatment.htm>

Website ban covers 50,000 sites, group claims. 4 Feb. 2009. <http://www.bangkokpost.com/news/local/136219/website-ban-covers-50000-sites-group-claims>

Morgan, D. Megan's Law No Deterrent To Sex Offenders. 6 Feb. 2009. <http://www.cbsnews.com/stories/2009/02/06/national/main4780981.shtml>

CDC: Obesity Prevalence. 10 Feb. 2009. <http://www.cdc.gov/nccdphp/dnpa/obesity/childhood/prevalence.htm>

ScienceDaily: Talking and Treating Erectile Dysfunction. 14 Feb. 2009. <http://www.sciencedaily.com/releases/2009/02/090204172216.htm>

National Center for Learning Disabilities. 14 March 2009. <http://www.ncld. org/content/view/605/>

National Organic Program. 20 March 2009. <http://www.ams.usda.gov/ AMSv1.0/ams.fetchTemplateData.do?template=TemplateA&navID=N ationalOrganicProgram&leftNav=NationalOrganicProgram&page=N OPNationalOrganicProgramHome&acct=nop>

Issues About Change: Inclusion: The Pros and Cons. (1995). Retrieved on 22 March 2009 from the Southwestern Educational Development Laboratory website: <http://www.sedl.org/change/issues/issues43.html>

University of Utah (2009, January 3). Car Key Jams Teen Drivers' Cell Phones. *ScienceDaily*. Retrieved 23 March 2009 from <http://www. sciencedaily.com /releases/2008/12/081231131218.htm>

Club drugs linked to sexual assaults, serious health effects. 26 March 2009. <http://www.hazelden.org/web/public/ade00131.page>

Marijuana: Facts Parents Need to Know. 26 March 2009. <http://www.nida. nih.gov/MarijBroch/parentpg9-10N.html#Effects

Talking With Kids About Drugs. 26 March 2009. <http://www.healthieryou. com/kidsdrugs.html>

Government and Industry Responses to Media Violence. 28 March 2009. <http://www.media-awareness.ca/english/issues/violence/govt_ industry_responses.cfm>

NetSmartz Workshop. 28 March 2009. <http://www.netsmartz.org/index. aspx>

The Youth Violence Epidemic. 28 March 2009. <http://www.apa.org/ppo/ issues/pbviolence.html> Suicide- New World Encyclopedia. 28 March 2009. <http://www.newworldencyclopedia.org/entry/Suicide>

Your Child & A Healthy Lifestyle. 28 March 2009. <http://www.tricycletour. co.za/advice.aspx> Fox, K. (1997). Mirror, mirror: A summary of research findings on body image. 28 March 2009. <http://www.sirc.org/publik/ mirror.html>

Environmental Working Group. 31 March 2009. <http://www.foodnews. org/fulllist.php>

What is Zen Buddhism? 19 April 2009. <http://www.enotes.com/history- fact-finder/religion/what-zen-Buddhism>

Printed in the United States
221919BV00004B/1/P

9 781440 153037